MW01293783

TALES OF THE INTRACOASTAL WATERWAY

An Account of a Passage from the Florida Keys to Cape Cod on a Seventeen Foot Catboat

Roland Sawyer Barth

The Catboat Association Press

authorHOUSE®

AuthorHouse™
1663 Liberty Drive
Bloomington, IN 47403
www.authorhouse.com
Phone: 1-800-839-8640

First published by AuthorHouse 1/21/2010

ISBN: 978-1-4490-5393-2 (e)
ISBN: 978-1-4490-5391-8 (sc)

Library of Congress Control Number: 2009913753

Printed in the United States of America
Bloomington, Indiana

This book is printed on acid-free paper.

There lies the boat, there blows the morning breeze.
It is a point of honor, now, to go.

E.B. White, *The Sea and the Wind that Blows*

The Voyage of IBIS

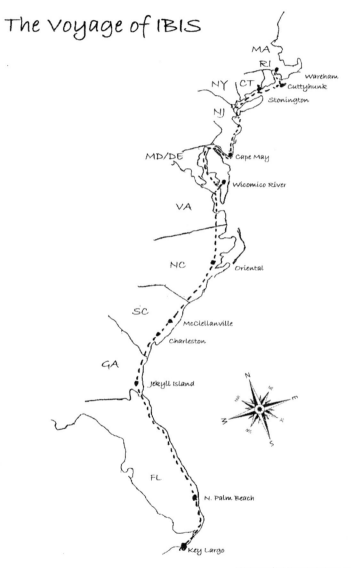

MA

RI

NY CT

Wareham

Cuttyhunk

Stonington

NJ

MD/DE

Cape May

Wicomico River

VA

NC

Oriental

SC

McClellanville

Charleston

GA

Jekyll Island

FL

N. Palm Beach

Key Largo

N

S

E

W

Chart Copyright 2009; Barbara Bauman & Roland Barth

Foreword

As a life-long sailor and one who has read Catboat Association (CBA) Bulletins from near the beginning of the organization, I have always envied those who reported tales of their long-distance voyages on small boats. Whether I was sailing my parents' Dyer dhow, skipping along waves on a windsurfer or passing a lazy afternoon at the helm of the family's Marshall catboat, *Red Squirrel*, I dreamed of long distance voyages and when I might be able to do the same.

When presented with an early manuscript of Roland's voyage by Charlie Ladoulis, a fellow catboat sailor, I knew immediately that we had to somehow become involved in publishing this 21st century version of *The Boy, Me and the Cat* by Henry M. Plummer. Mr. Plummer sailed the same waters, south and back again, with his son and a cat, approximately 100 years prior and lived to tell the tale. He distributed typewritten accounts of his own journey and later the CBA published the same text with photos of the journey.

Mr. Barth's tale is a wonderful narration of the same journey (though only one direction) with friends, relatives and often the companionship of seabirds alone. I am pleased to help share the log of his joys and struggles of the journey up the Intracoastal Waterway in a 17' catboat, *Ibis*. Enjoy the ride!

- Tim Lund, President, *The Catboat Association*

Front and Rear Cover Photos by Rose Thompson

Catboat Silhouette by Jon Luoma

Production Editor: John Conway

Introduction

Some years ago---never mind how long precisely---having little or no money in my purse, and nothing particular to interest me on shore, I thought I would sail about a little and see the watery part of the world. It is a way I have of driving off the spleen, and regulating the circulation. Whenever I find myself growing grim about the mouth; whenever it is a damp, drizzle November in my soul; whenever I find myself involuntarily pausing before coffin warehouses and bringing up the rear of every funeral I meet; and especially whenever my hypos get such an upper hand of me, that it requires a strong moral principle to prevent me from deliberately stepping into the street, and methodically knocking people's hats off---then, I account it high time to get to the sea as soon as I can. This is my substitute for pistol and ball. With a philosophical flourish Cato throws himself upon his sword; I quietly take to the ship.

-Herman Melville, *Moby-Dick*

Most of my sailing life has taken place along the coast of Maine aboard a 1911 Friendship Sloop. It wasn't until a few years ago, having taken up winter residence in the Florida Keys, that I discovered another gaff-rigged vessel. My wife and I purchased from a neighbor a shallow draft, 17-foot Cape Cod Catboat so we could sail Florida Bay. We were now handsomely prepared to explore the very skinny, little known, 850 square miles of the wondrous Everglades National Park.

Ibis and litter of catboats in the Everglades. Photo by Rose Thompson

We christened our catboat *Ibis*. Pronounced ahy-bis, an ibis is a breathtakingly lovely, snow-white wading bird with black wing tips and a long down curved bill. Related to herons and storks, it is found in tropical regions. The ibis is the mascot chosen by the University of Miami because of its legendary bravery during hurricanes. You see, ibis are the last wildlife to take shelter before a hurricane and the first to reappear once the storm has passed.

Because we frequently find ourselves out before, during and after storms on Florida Bay, we felt this lovely bird should be our mascot as well.

We soon discovered just how much fun these little catboats are to sail and how able they are in shoal waters. And I continue to discover just how special are those who sail them. Before long, I discovered *The Boy, Me and the Cat*, a charming account written by Henry Plummer of his 1912 voyage along the coast from Cape Cod to Miami ... and back.

Like most catboaters who revel in this remarkable story, I began to fantasize about making the trip myself. Hey, if Henry Plummer could do it when there *was* no Intracoastal Waterway, surely I could do it in a well-marked, dredged channel with a modern engine, plentiful marinas, a GPS … and Sea Tow. Surely.

The fantasy continued to haunt and provoke me until, one day, pondering the impending turn of my odometer to 70 years of age, I decided to convince myself that I still had a pulse and some nautical miles left under my keel. I would "quietly take to the ship."

Our mascot.

An adventure has been defined as "an experience the outcome of which you do not know in advance." I decided to give myself as a birthday present an adventure of many weeks and about 2200 miles sailing *Ibis* from the Florida Keys back to her birthplace in Wareham, Buzzards Bay, on Cape Cod. And, not incidentally, sailing myself from Florida back in time to my own place of birth seven decades before in nearby Boston.

What follows is an account of the planning and preparation for, conduct of and reflection upon this adventure. These words are drawn from my electronic correspondence with family and friends during the passage. I hope that, just as Henry Plummer's passage got me thinking and sailing, my own story will invite you, dear reader, to participate in this adventure up the coast from a chair beside the fire. Or better, that it will provoke *you* to take to the ship!

Finally, let me add that most of what you are about to read is true … at least to the extent my ageing, porous mind can accurately recall and recapture what happened. All photographs are taken by the skipper unless otherwise indicated.

To embellish and enrich the account … and to keep me honest … I have invited the crewmembers that shared in this adventure to add a few words of their own.

Enjoy the voyage!

Fair winds and fond wishes,
Roland Sawyer Barth
Key Largo, Florida

Chapter 1
An Invitation to a
70th Birthday Party

February 7, 2007

Florida Keys

Dear friends,

For perhaps 50 years I've sailed the waters of Maine. And for another 20 years, the waters of Florida. This spring I'm planning to give myself a two and a half month, 70th birthday present: I want to fulfill my lifetime dream and sail the waters *between* Florida and New England.

Now this is not as foolhardy and unprecedented an idea as it may seem. For in 1912, one Henry Plummer, accompanied by a young boy and a scruffy cat, sailed *Mascot*, his substantial 24' catboat from New Bedford, Massachusetts to Miami, Florida and back. This adventure is suitably memorialized as *The Boy, Me and the Cat*.

By the way, the boy and "me" made it. Alas, the cat did not withstand the journey. Its future was portended by this entry in the log, the night before they all set out: "Crawled under the shed, caught the cat, rubbed her full of flea powder, and dropped her into a gunny sack to moult. Will have troubles enough without fleas."

Having sufficiently whetted your appetite let me say that, nearly a hundred years after Plummer, there may be a sack for *you* on this forthcoming passage!

Over my lifetime I have discovered a number of friends ... a small number to be sure ... who have demonstrated the peculiar capacity to live with me in close quarters aboard ship for extended periods of time. This involves, of course, suspension of normal conversational etiquette, of edible cuisine, of sanitary hygiene, and of the conventional fulfillment of bodily functions. All of these are sacrificed to a higher good: "the boys' night on the town."

Your name has been put forth for consideration by an anonymous acquaintance. I suspect a week is the longest you and I could live in relentless intimacy without resorting to floggings, mutiny ... or cannibalism. Probably three or four days is the shortest period that would warrant the considerable travel involved. If you would like to contemplate "quietly taking to the ship" with me for a portion of this voyage, read on. If not ... well, read on anyway!

I plan to depart the Florida Keys around the first of April. My hoped-for landfall around mid June will be at the Cape Cod Shipbuilding Company in Wareham, Buzzards Bay, Massachusetts. This yard, in continuous operation since 1899, is where *Ibis*, my 17-foot Cape Cod Catboat, was constructed many years ago. And from whence it will be shipped back to Florida.

You may express ... or decline ... an interest by letting me know:

a) "Thanks but no thanks. 17 feet is too small for two people, with or without a cat, particularly when one of them is *you*, Roland!"

b) "I will think about it for a while and get back to you."

c) "I am interested in considering shipping on during the following window of days" (e.g. between May 1-15).

d) "I am interested in considering a passage with you and *Ibis* over this piece of water:" (e.g. the Georgia coast)

e)   "Sign me onto the ship's manifest!"

I will then take inventory of candidates, times, dates, and waters and put together some sort of (dare I say) plan. In the unlikely event of an overwhelming outpouring of interest it may not be possible to accommodate everyone or everyone's preference. In that case you can all take the boat and I'll take the train!

A difficult part of all of this will be your travel: getting from where you are to where *Ibis* is; and then, a few days later, getting from where *Ibis* and you will be, to where you want to be. Because of winds, weather, tides and currents, I cannot know in advance where *Ibis* will be, nor when. These uncertain conditions may involve some last minute plane reservations, car rentals, pick up at airports, or … who knows what. But I am certain it can be done, if not always easily.

Friends are the first to pledge dollars to support our march for hunger, AIDS, or a healthy heart. In this spirit, my good seafaring wife Barbara has demonstrated leadership *and courage* by signing on for the first leg from Key Largo to West Palm Beach. But there are conditions. She reserves the right to put in for daily showers, or to jump ship before or during this passage. And, come hell or high water … or both … she *will* fly back to Boston on April 16th to her work at the Brigham and Women's Hospital. In short, Barbara will be at the West Palm Airport on Sunday afternoon … no matter where *Ibis* and I are. So much for my cardinal, longstanding rule of cruising: "Never let anyone on board who has to get *off* board at a given time or place!"

What about you?

I look forward with interest, anticipation … and amusement … to what comes next.

Fair winds and fond wishes,
Roland

Chapter 2
Full Disclosure

February 15th

Florida Keys

Dear family and friends,

Since our last correspondence much has happened. Let me bring you up to date.

The Intracoastal Waterway (ICW) Trip is definitely *on*. *Ibis* and I will depart the Keys on April 12th, (weather permitting). Barbara has not wavered, and so for four days she will be the first crewmember from Key Largo to about West Palm Beach (Barbara permitting).

Others have tactfully declined my invitation to avail themselves of this opportunity. A host of inventive reasons have been offered.

Six of you, from all over the country, have indicated a *definite* wish to ship on. Perhaps another half dozen are "thinking it over."

I'm overwhelmed and heartened by this display of interest ... and mettle! Since I expect this passage to take about 10 weeks, clearly I will have ample company! I hope, although cannot guarantee, that if you want some days aboard you shall have them. I really look forward to that.

I'll be in touch with each of you, individually, to see if we can get our windows to open simultaneously. This exercise will challenge my rusty administrative skills, last employed by this principal when scheduling a school of 500 kids and 40 teachers in classes for the year! I should have things sorted out around mid-March ... both my end and your end.

Some of you (unlike me) have real jobs and must schedule specific days. Others will be scheduling by sections of the ICW you would particularly like to travel. The former are easier to schedule with certainty than the latter. Ultimately, of course, it will come down to dates not places.

My good wife (who knows first hand about these things) has encouraged me to provide some truth in advertising, about what your participation will entail. So let me try and give you an honest appraisal fully realizing that I've never been there nor done that.

I'll be subscribing to the belt and suspenders school of seamanship. We'll carry an extra sail in case one shreds. We'll carry an extra engine in case one fails. There is a 15 hp inboard saildrive. In addition, I'll hang over the transom a new 6 hp outboard. Expect *lots* of motoring, so two engines seem prudent, even on a sailboat. And we'll carry two large anchors. You never know.

There are tides of 3 to 8 feet in the Intracoastal, less in North Carolina where they are much reduced by the Outer Banks. There are strong currents, especially under bridges, and around the rivers and inlets from the Atlantic.

Ibis draws 2 feet. There is pretty much certainty of 6 feet of water in the ICW, usually more. But you never know. Maintenance of navigation aids and dredging have been lax of late. So if one sails or wanders or is swept off course, danger of grounding looms. If the bottom is soft, this entails muddy feet. If the bottom is rocky, this may entail an unaccustomed vocabulary. You never know.

At times there will be lots of traffic and wake, mostly from motorboats. They will be trying harder to avoid the shoals than they will to avoid us. But there are also lots of beautiful, quiet, out of the way stretches.

Weather (but I hope not interpersonal) conditions will vary from superb to miserable. I've selected this time of year to follow spring north so it shouldn't be too hot or cold. But you never know. Going north, the sun will be behind us most of the time, for ease in viewing wildlife, other boats, and navigation aides. But the sun will be strong. Provision accordingly. A small Bimini can cover some of the cockpit. Prevailing winds should be southerly. But you never know.

Probably best to check in with me on my weather before you leave home. If the upcoming few days promise rain, come a few days later (see "close quarters" below). It's possible your entire booking could be washed out.

When conditions are favorable (direction and velocity of winds, or no winds) we'll probably sail, motor-sail or motor for long days. This can be very wearing ... in lots of ways.

Close quarters. With such a small vessel on so many large waters, I expect to be a "fair weather sailor" and not try to buck strong tides, seas, headwinds, rains ... or closed bridges. We will be heading northeast so, for instance, a nor'easter will shut things down for a few days. This will mean lots of anchoring and waiting.

When waiting out these adverse elements the choices are two: be confined to a very small cabin (with me!) or go ashore. I'll be towing a little 8-foot kayak as a dinghy, not good for paddling in a blow ... especially for two. So the former alternative may prevail. I have reading lights and lots of nautical literature on board.

Bunks are six feet and spacious, a blessing of this beamy catboat.

Storage is very limited and will be occupied by lots of gear. So one soft duffel is the maximum allowed by this carrier ... and by Homeland Security.

We'll be stopping at marinas for fuel, food, and showers from time to time as conditions allow and need demands. There are many of them on the ICW.

Food. Ah, food! I will provide all the food. I'll be carrying a large, super-insulated cooler, a one-burner alcohol stove, and a few plates and pieces of eating ware. Bad news: chow will be modest (except what you cook); good news: everything tastes better at sea (even what I cook!) Please advise me of unusual dietary needs.

On the other end of things: the porta-potti. This device is very closely integrated with the bunkroom ... in fact the feet of the sleeping bags converge with the toilet lid. Forget privacy ... and modesty! Methane is best emitted on deck. Relieve yourself thoroughly before you leave home.

I am able and quite willing to solo for long periods of time. I enjoy it. This means that you can cancel your "reservation" at any time without leaving me high and dry, as it were. Clearly the more notice the better as it will allow me to plan and to accommodate others. Given the numbers involved here, it's unlikely that I'll be able to "re-book" you. But you never know. Once we are underway, like Barbara, you reserve the right to conclude your passage (jump ship!) at any time for any reason. Reasons need not be disclosed. In fact, in deference to our future relationship, reasons probably should *not* be disclosed!

This full disclosure should give you sufficient information to help you make a decision. Truth in Advertising. I hope I have not deterred too many!

Keep me posted on your plans as your life unfolds. I shall do the same.

Fair winds and fond wishes,
Roland

Chapter 3
Packin' Up

April 2nd

Florida Keys

Dear family, friends and crewmembers,

The page in the calendar has turned to April and the time to cast off the dock lines is rapidly approaching.

Barbara will arrive in five days. After a couple of days packing and provisioning, we intend to embark on the 10th, weather permitting.

The weather has not been permitting much these past few weeks. It's been blowing strong, 20-25 knots, and from the northeast, not favorable winds for a trip up the ICW in a small vessel. I'm hoping for a change soon to the southeasterlies, more common for this time of year.

A few words by way of helping you to prepare and pack up:

Space is *very* tight and getting tighter all the time.

I have a duffel bag, about 24" long and 12" in diameter. It just fits in the port cockpit locker (along with one of the anchors, the fuel can, engine oil, mooring pole, paddle, extra rope, and lines!). That's all I intend to bring for clothes for the duration. You will have the starboard cockpit locker and should try hard to confine yourself to the same dimensions. You are also allowed a small backpack to be stowed in the cabin. Sharing your cockpit locker will be all of our *food*. Take your pick!

The art form for small boat cruising is, of course, not to bring anything you don't absolutely have to; and to bring everything you do absolutely have to.

I have, and you do *not* need to bring:

a) Foul weather suit
b) Food and water
c) Reading materials
d) Sun lotion
e) Bug repellent

You *should* bring:

a) One suit of cold weather clothes, Polartec is much better than cotton or wool
b) Two hot weather outfits: a brimmed hat, a long shirt and long pants for sun protection
c) A towel
d) A toilet kit, which includes all-important medicines. Geriatrics must only hope that these will not completely occupy the duffel!
e) One pair of shoes with soft, not-black, soles. Docksiders or sneakers are best.
f) A small flashlight (I have reading lights).

I anticipate lots of reading time in the likely event of unfavorable weather, waiting for bridges to open, or evening enjoyment. A great bibliography I have been working my way through this winter includes these three, all of which will be aboard, in the ship's library. They are also at Amazon.com.

a) *The Boy, Me and the Cat*, by Henry Plummer, available from The Catboat Association, Inc, PO Box 72, Middleboro, MA 02346. This delightful little volume is what inspired me to make this trip. It's an absorbing account almost a century ago of the author sailing/motoring his catboat from Cape Cod to Miami before there was an Intracoastal Waterway. And then he and his son turned around and sailed *back* to New England! In order to make our time aboard feel plush and easy, this is an "assigned reading."

b) *The Biggest Boat I Could Afford: Sailing up the US Coast in a Dinghy*, by Lee Hughes, Sheridan House. This is the account of a chap from New Zealand who decided to sail from the Keys to Maine in a 16-foot open dinghy with a 3 hp engine … so that he could learn how to sail and overcome his fear of water! An engaging read which demonstrates both bravery and folly … virtues with which we will undoubtedly become familiar. He didn't make it.

c) *The Inside Passage*, by Anthony Bailey, McMillan. Written by a *New Yorker* writer, this is the story of the author and a handful of others motoring up the ICW from Daytona Beach to the Chesapeake on a substantial powerboat. Lots of good side trips and photos. A lyrical and aesthetic experience that ably demonstrates the *other* way to make a passage up the ICW … your second trip, perhaps!

And then, allow me to suggest:

d) *Cruising Rules: Relationship at Sea*, available from this author at RSB44@aol.com. This is a collection of sailing stories from the Coast of Maine and Florida with accompanying "cruising rules," compliance with which purports to ensure that two people will get along harmoniously in relentless intimacy for long periods on a small boat. We'll see!

Roland and Barbara casting off from the dock on Key Largo. Photo by Alice Arakelian.

That's it for this sitting.

No cancellations yet! Keep focused … and committed. Let me know your plan and any questions. Communication will be very haphazard after *Ibis* leaves this dock next week.

Fair winds and fond wishes,
Roland

Chapter 4
The Week in Review

April 16th

North Palm Beach, FL

Dear family and friends,

Because an account from a former crewmember is probably more useful and creditable to a future crewmember than the Official Account prepared by the Captain, I have invited Barbara to author the "log" of our first leg up the ICW. Here's what you can look forward to:

> As I write this, I'm sitting in the cockpit of *Ibis*. It's blowing a fairly strong breeze from some direction (I'm only modestly proficient with knots of wind speed and directions of the compass). Tonight, Saturday, is my last night aboard, as I am booked to fly out of West Palm Beach at noon tomorrow, to return to that other life in Boston.
>
> As Roland's first-rate first mate, I'd like to offer a few comments to the story of the journey so far. It has been a very full week, and those of you who plan to join Roland at some future date may be especially interested in my experience.

Roland, Barbara and *Ibis*. Photo by Rose Thompson.

We've had some gorgeous sunny days with perfect wind. Earlier in the week, after a long day underway, we anchored in the lee of a little island off Miami Harbor, both of us really hot and sweaty, and jumped into the cool salt water. Totally refreshing and sublime. After a delicious supper heated on the one-burner alcohol stove and a nice glass of wine, we crashed into our bunks and slept soundly. Until ...

A brutal thunderstorm with heavy gusts of wind arrived in the wee morning hours. The anchor dragged, we were about to go aground, so of course we had to climb out of dry sleeping bags, naked as jaybirds, crawl onto the wet, pitching deck, and reset the anchor. Roland ran the engine; I ran the anchor! The event was well illuminated by continuous, violent lightning strikes! No hands on the wire forestay.

Another rainy day was passed in Ft. Lauderdale, where we spent the day at the city marina. *Ibis* would hardly qualify as a proper dinghy-on-davits on some of those motor yachts. We walked around town until the rains let up. Other than that, it has been pretty hot and sunny. We've stayed at three lovely anchorages and three marinas.

Thanks to our dear friends Ruth and Harry back in the Keys, we've had fabulous dinners every night. Ruth's *bon voyage* gift to us was a freezer full of homemade stew, chili, spaghetti sauce, and shrimp Creole. Our cooler kept things nice and chilled. Sorry, though, we've pretty much finished off all these goodies. Roland's meal plan from hereon is canned goods ... except he promises to have fresh salad regularly. Perhaps he will catch fish from time to time. Those joining him in the future should know that the galley is well equipped with everything necessary to cook real food, including a great little pressure cooker. All you will need is real food!

The surgical nurse sterilizing the dishes.

As for the sailing itself, we've come about 150 miles in 6 days. We cast off from the dock in Key Largo on Monday the 10th and sailed from the Keys, across Biscayne Bay and into Miami. After that, lots of motoring, some sailing, some motor sailing.

Roland and I agree that the sailing conditions have been more challenging than either of us anticipated. Most daunting has been the huge amount of powerboat traffic. Many of these boats are absolutely enormous. All move fast, and most are completely unconcerned with their large effect on a small sailboat.

The winds in the ICW always seem to be on the nose or off the stern. This week has served up heavy following winds which mean the reefed sail is out full on a run most of the time. And finally, there are many, many bridges across the ICW that are too low for us to pass under. This means you have to wait until the bridge tender opens the bridge, which can be 10-30 minutes, depending on schedules. A real drag, and especially challenging if you arrive at them with the full sail out and no room to head up into the wind!

A few other highlights:

Sailing past mansion after mansion after mansion and enormous yacht after enormous yacht between Miami and West Palm Beach. It's said that Miami is where the millionaires go. And that the billionaires go to Ft. Lauderdale. Something is wrong when so many spend so much on these things.

Sailing through Port Everglades (Ft. Lauderdale) and Lake Worth (West Palm Beach) ... some of the tensest, hairiest times we've ever had in a sailboat. The maritime version of spaghetti junction. Currents, winds, bridges, traffic.

Swimming in the ocean at Delray Beach, my favorite beach so far. Very modest, but great sand and fabulous clear water, shaded from yellow green to turquoise to cobalt blue. We walked in the evening through the neighborhood, which looked like a postcard from the 50's: low, candy-colored houses, lots of bougainvillea and hibiscus. Then, up early the next morning to watch the sun rise over the ocean. Lovely.

Finding out that the last two marinas we stayed at had swimming pools and swimming at the end of the day.

Seeing flocks of real ibis flying over our *Ibis* in Miami Harbor.

So, many hits, some misses, a few strikeouts, but, overall, an auspicious beginning for the great adventure!

And, as always, looking forward to lots of conversation with you all after it's over. Your turn next!

Fair winds, Barbara

Before she left, Barbara bestowed upon me a most valuable gift: two check lists, drawn up with all of the precision, anticipation and planning of a surgical nurse.

Barbara, after the frist leg heading back to Boston. (Note equiptment...and smile!)

The first: "Before checking out of a marina." At these infrequent, perhaps weekly, stops it is critical not to depart, get back on the waterway and then remember, "Oh damn … " So, don't forget to:

a) Replenish all fuel tanks
b) Replenish ice and water
c) Refill sunshower

d) Replenish food and drink
e) Charge batteries
  VHF radio for bridges
  Ship's battery
  Computer battery
  Video and still cameras
  Nickel cadmium batteries for headlamps, etc.
f) Do laundry
g) Send e-mails

The second list proved even more important for use on a daily basis during my single-handed days when, in the midst of wakes from other vessels, narrow passes, gusty winds and ever-present navigation aids, it is virtually impossible to leave or lash the tiller and go below to rummage about looking for … whatever. So,

a) Make lunch and put in cockpit in little cooler
b) Water container accessible
c) Grapefruit peeled
d) Prescription reading and dark glasses in cockpit
e) Apply sunscreen
f) Marine radio and charts and cruising guides in cockpit
g) Inflatable life vest and life harness in cockpit
h) Fill outboard tank with fuel
i) Secure all deck lashing: two anchors at the bow, sunshower, paddle, kayak
j) Check bilge for water
k) Cover cooler below with cushions

No idiot could forget these things … but of course I could! Thanks for these parting gifts, Barbara!

Fair winds and fond wishes,
Roland

Chapter 5
Bruising Water

April 28th

Jekyll Island, GA

Dear family and friends,

Florida has what seems like a never-ending coast. But *Ibis* has crossed her first state line and now rests at a slip in the Jekyll Harbor Marina in *Georgia*! We have covered just about ¼ of the distance to Cape Cod.

Much to report.

Barbara got off at North Palm Beach after a good week at sea. We're still talking to one another! She has been a good-natured, first-rate, first mate … midnight anchor relocation in the tropical downpour, notwithstanding. Since her departure, standards set by the surgical nurse have fallen a bit. Instead of a fresh water rinse, soap wash and another fresh water rinse, the procedure for dishes has been modified to a salt-water rinse and a fresh water chaser. The porta-potti has seen considerably less use and meals are a bit more "basic."

For some reason, inexplicable to Barbara when I agreed to it, and inexplicable to me now, I had committed to giving workshops to two groups of Florida educators in the Palm Beach area on my passage through. What was I *thinking*?

What I was thinking was that it might provide a welcome interruption from life on the water to "take a day off." I could sleep in a real and stable bed, eat a couple of solid meals, take some showers, enjoy a real flush, and help finance my passage up the ICW. And maybe even provide some useful counsel to these good school folks. My hosts had agreed to pick me up anywhere within range of Palm Beach and drive me to the sites. Made sense ... back then.

But now I had to stand and deliver. I faced several problems: I had secured my notes and overheads in a waterproof plastic bag in the bilges. Happily, I discovered them, safe and dry. But I couldn't uncover any socks or undershorts or a shirt that might accept a necktie. Or a necktie. No wonder there was so much room in that little duffel! A couple of phone calls brought assurance from my bemused host that he would secure and bring the necessary items to the dock where I would properly "suit up."

The bigger problem was that, after a week in the hot sun and strong winds dodging powerboats, day markers, shoals, and bridge abutments, my head was awash. Improving public schools couldn't be further from what was left of my mind. My retrieval system for wise words and ideas was nowhere within reach. Nonetheless, I proceeded, hoping that that other life would miraculously "cut in" during my introduction. So, somewhat cleaned up and rested from a night in a hotel and suited in some unfamiliar, albeit clean, duds, it was off to a morning with the principals of the Palm Beach Schools and an afternoon with the faculty of a Vero Beach school.

It was a day to remember. Only I can't remember it! Somehow, after about a half hour of sleepwalking, I switched from navigating the ICW on an unsteady platform, without the benefit of an autopilot, over to educator-on-autopilot on a firmer podium. I managed to get through the day. Some bravery and much folly! I learned that one cannot trifle in either piloting a small boat or public speaking by blending one with the other. They entail different skill sets, different costumes, and different frames of mind. From now on, until I reach Cape Cod, I swear I will stow the educator hat and wear only that of the seaman. One hat at a time is all I can manage these days … if that.

My good friend Geoff Cook came on board on Saturday a few miles north of Vero Beach. I was relieved that he had read and was thoroughly versed in *The Boy, Me and the Cat* that I had decided to mail ahead to each forthcoming crewmember. Everyone would know what lay ahead … while there was still time to back out!

Geoff departed this afternoon after a full 7 days of wonderful winds and currents. On his watch we covered 264 miles, an average of about 38 miles per day. This was partially due to long days of 7am departures and 6pm arrivals, but also to very strong following winds. In fact, yesterday breezes were so strong we could no longer hold a double reef and had to motor in 25-30 knots on the transom. Average speed for the week was about 5 knots, which is booking for *Ibis*!

We took turns at the tiller, at the chart, at the binoculars, and occasionally, when things got confusing, at the GPS.

We anchored most nights, frequently in uncharted nooks and crannies, often amidst a curious assortment of beached, wrecked and abandoned vessels. The procedure: Geoff would get in the kayak and "sound" a passage in with his paddle-depthfinder. If he could find 2 feet, allowing for tide, then I motored *Ibis* in behind. If not then we looked elsewhere. When he didn't pilot us in we usually found bottom and one of us (him) had to go over the side and push us off.

In St. Augustine we laid over for two hours in front of Castillo San Marcos, constructed by the Spanish in 1565, where we waited for the tide to go slack at the Inlet. I had last visited this fort with my parents some 60 years ago! This layover enabled us to avoid the current and sand shoals and get safely across. While we waited we saw a large, deep draft sloop, not so fortunate. It grounded and, with a dreadful heel, was swept over the bar and out to sea. Just a reminder … as if we needed one. Then we spent a fine night at a marina on the north shore of the inlet. The stop also included an instructive walk about America's oldest city and fort, and a wonderful meal at a restaurant under live oaks and Spanish moss with Kaki and JP, good friends from Maine.

Geoff on "depthsounding" mission.

Then it was time to move on and "bruise some water," as Henry Plummer put it.

There are many signs that we are moving north:

Chimneys! Don't have many of these in the Keys.
Live oaks and southern pines replacing the palms.
Rocks, replacing mud and sand.

In addition, the number of dolphins has become remarkable. They seem to be more prevalent, playful, and present than mosquitoes ... which on their part *are* prevalent, playful and present. Six or eight dolphins joined Geoff and me for dinner at anchor last night off the Cape Canaveral Canal in the company of some eerie shipwrecks.

And the challenges continue: especially running downwind in a good blow, with sail out full, around serpentine turns frequently necessitating either heavy-air gybes or tacking with limited room on the shore.

And the bridges. The charts don't show all of the most recent fixed replacements, all at a standard 65-foot clearance, necessary for securing federal funding. The small community of diminishing bridge tenders refers dismissively to these new structures as "high-rise bridges." These are easy for us to get under but, because bridges are built across narrows, they often harbor some wicked currents. The guidebook says of the Atlantic Avenue Bridge south of Fernandina that we managed yesterday: "Caution: currents are very swift at this bridge. The ebb flows at 5.5 knots." *We* motor, at best, 4 to 5 knots. We got up in the dark and passed under, near slack.

And the inlets. As we head north we continue to also try to take these at slack, as we did the Matanzas and Ponce de Leon inlets in the past couple of days. The best slack is slack low. This assures that the currents are with us as we head towards the inlet while the waters flow out to sea ... and with us as we head north away from the inlet when the tide begins to come back in. The slack high is the reverse: against us on both sides of the inlet. Periodic cell phone calls to Barbara in Boston the night before supplied times of slack high and low ... thanks to the internet.

Ferocious currents at inlets and bridges frequently require *both* engines ("twin screws", one crewmember called them) going at full steam *and* sail power to maintain control and make any headway ... such as under the bascule bridge, a hinged bridge split at the center, we came under yesterday at the St. John's River.

And lots and *lots* of renumbered, reset, removed, and additional navigation aids, which the charts, of course, don't show. Hence the help of the GPS from time to time to ensure us that we are where we *think* we are.

But, of course, that's half the pleasure and satisfaction of all of this: successfully negotiating these unpredictable predicaments ... so far.

Here's how Geoff recalls our time together:

> Foremost in my mind about my time aboard this wonderful catboat - the privilege of being there. *Ibis*, while not big, provided a comfortable home and a terrific sailing experience. Her able and affable skipper and beautiful surroundings made for a rare treat. For the most part, winds were favorable and we were under sail. The white knuckle moments came on runs at the edge of a gybe (I was a rookie dealing with and reefing that big main) or getting past half-open bascule bridges with more wind or current than we would have liked.
>
> I shed rookie status as a kayaker when the captain would send me ahead of *Ibis* in our red kayak seeking a channel for nighttime anchorages in attractive and secluded gunk holes. Meals were a delight —I enjoyed them all. Invariably breakfasts happened during Florida sunrises; dinners included a glass or two of wine and memorable sunsets.
>
> As we proceeded, I was struck by the changing scene ... rocks along the shore instead of sand; pin oaks and Spanish moss appeared. I had never seen such flights of ibis, white herons, and roseate spoonbills along with pelicans coming in to their rookery near one of our anchorages. All unforgettable.
>
> But the best part: the fellowship. There was ample time for real conversation. I recall a warm and moving chat about our daughters followed by a toast. Hours of talking and listening during one of those rare opportunities to give voice to opinions, aspirations, and concerns led to subjects I had hitherto discussed with no one. Roland is not only a fine sailor, but a dear and trusted friend.

Ninety-five years earlier Henry Plummer, his son and his cat made a similar voyage. I can't imagine that his experience was any richer than mine.

Geoffrey B. Cooke
Franklin, Tennessee

This afternoon, April 28th, James Asheton-Miller, a long-time dear friend, flew into Jacksonville from Ann Arbor Michigan, rented a car and drove here to Jekyll Island to come aboard. Geoff returned James' rental car to the Jacksonville Airport where some friends (who had driven him to Vero Beach) delivered his car. The first successful, inventive, logistical maneuver of the trip!

Now we're about to go off to *suppah* at a very local Georgia restaurant here at the Marina … if they let us in. You see, James was severely reprimanded earlier in the day for walking through the dining room carrying a loaded … porta-potti! Ah, the humiliation a crewmember must endure!

Fair winds and fond wishes,
Roland

Chapter 6
Low Country

May 5th

Charleston, SC

Dear family and friends,

I write from the dock at the Charleston City Marina. South Carolina: another state!

Well, my needs for boats and boating are being fully met ... and then some!

Ibis and I have come about 700 miles from the Florida Keys ... with about 1500 to go to Cape Cod. I am exhilarated ... and exhausted. Exhilarated by the remarkable and always changing and unfolding ICW. Exhausted from long days in frequently high and following winds and seas.

Some observations from the low country of coastal Georgia and South Carolina:

Whoever chose the names of rivers, creeks, streams, sounds and bays had a good imagination ... and sense of humor: Rockdedundy River, Julienton River, Old Teakettle Creek, Dog Hammer Spit, Buttermilk

Sound. These waterways meander in tortuous turns with shoals on one side and mud on the other. The chart looks like an intestinal system gone haywire! We sail ten miles to make three good.

You never know what is around the next bend. For instance St. Catherine's Island is owned largely by the New York Zoological Association. Here they release for study zebras, wildebeest and other large African animals. Looked for, but didn't see any on our safari over this watery Serengeti!

The course has taken us inside the barrier islands. Besides St. Catherine's, there are Cumberland, Jekyll, St. Simon, and Sapelo Islands. Every day or two we negotiate huge sounds the size of Penobscot Bay in Maine. These are now traversed using GPS, as the currents are very strong, markers few, and the sand shoals abundant. It's very difficult to plot a good course by dead reckoning. My competence with, confidence in, and need for the GPS grows daily.

The natural wildlife is extraordinary. Huge flocks of all kinds of shore birds. And the dolphins. Much of the marshes happily remain National Wildlife Preserves.

When we come near land, live oaks and Spanish moss abound.

I am carrying on this journey several cruising guides, which, every day, have proven extremely useful. The most useful and engaging is the series written by Claiborne Young, available at the Salty Southeast Cruisers' Net, www.cruisingguide.com:

Guide to Eastern Florida
Guide to Coastal South Carolina and Georgia
Coastal North Carolina

James and I are reading the history of these barrier islands as we pass by. For instance on one island, Parson Thomas Bosomworth married an Indian girl and set up religion amongst the natives ... until he was ceremoniously consumed by them!

Huge fires, thick smoke, and low visibility in tinder-dry Georgia call forth Maine fog-navigating skills.

Insect life is abundant out in the marshes: green heads, and especially no-see-ums. Mosquito netting at night slows 'em down but clearly doesn't stop 'em.

New, southern-style McMansions with docks sometimes lead a quarter-mile over the mudflats to a puddle of shallow water.

Powerboats outnumber sail by about 100 to 1. The bridges and shoals see to that. Nobody *with* sails, sails … except *Ibis*. We've been seeing the same four sailing sloops from Canada almost every day. They are completing "the big loop" down the Mississippi, across the Gulf of Mexico to Florida and now up the East Coast to home. They put in earlier than we do each night and power past us again each morning.

Lots of military in the South. We sailed by Parris Island Marine base and under the landing pattern of a nearby air base. The F-16's contributed to our good winds.

My fine crew, James, has been a gift. We both have bad backs, so between us we have one functioning body. And one good mind … his! He says we are like 6'-3" stick figures as we try to negotiate the diminutive cabin and cockpit. But we have done so with great success, if not grace. For a few days we demonstrated an astonishing level of interdependent teamwork by sharing one pair of socks (the ones from my day as educator in Palm Beach) which got pretty ripe. But the sun was eluded and the insects thwarted, if not asphyxiated, one foot at a time until a walk to a Kmart mercifully replenished the supply. James is a mechanical engineer so every problem has been thoroughly analyzed … and fixed. Oil changes, filter changes, electric socket repair. The unfamiliar vocabulary, *torque*, *sheer stress*, *volt meter*, is becoming familiar to this educator.

We're still trying to figure out how best to handle the frequent and humongous wakes of passing powerboats. One of these nearly swamped us yesterday. We rolled over and took gallons of water in the cockpit. More serious, the wake of this particularly offensive and offending waterplow knocked the sunshower over the side and both anchors as well. Fortunately, the lashings held these dangling, precious articles from joining Davy Jones' Locker. More secure lashings after that.

Now, when the sail is up and we enjoy a fresh breeze, we take the wakes parallel and the full sail dampens their effect. When under power, we slow the outboard down and drive into the wakes as the prop comes out of water and whirs in the air. To deal with really behemoth wakes, we turn tail and scramble for the shore. ICW cruising rule: the bigger the boat passing us and the faster it is going, the more likely we will both be in a narrows or under a bridge!

"Stick figure" motoring to windward.

We try to cross the huge and dangerous sounds in the early morning before the winds and seas come up and try to use favorable currents. This is almost impossible.

Ten thousand sail trims a day, it seems, as we run through the serpentines. I'd say about ½ motoring, ¼ motor sailing and ¼ sailing is the norm thus far.

A great visit in Beaufort, South Carolina where we walked among lovely antebellum homes. Many of these were "summer homes" on the cool(er) coast where wealthy plantation owners enjoyed comfort and escaped malaria. Slaves and field bosses stayed inland and were not as fortunate.

James and I share a deep interest in the Civil War. We once visited Gettysburg together. Yesterday we took a tour boat out to Fort Sumter in Charleston Harbor, a moving visit to the site where the Civil War began. We learned that Abraham Lincoln was to give a speech here in 1865 honoring the retaking of this fort by the Union forces. Alas, at the last moment, the President chose to remain in Washington in order to attend a play at Ford's Theater. The rest is history.

Here's what my British friend James has to add to the account:

> An enduring memory I shall cherish is sailing through the miles of serpentines in Georgia's salt marshes, through what seemed like an ocean of undulating waves of cord grass. Quiet and pristine, one half expected a dinosaur to emerge were it not for the occasional channel marker supporting a bald eagle's nest and the dolphins playing alongside. Some days we hailed but half a dozen boats. I remain inspired to think how far-sighted folks fought so successfully to protect this wonderful coastal region and its wildlife.
>
> One morning we weighed anchor at the crack of dawn in order to reach a bascule bridge in time for its first opening of the day at 7am. With 15 minutes to go we spotted the bridge 400 yards away across a meadow, and radioed the bridge tender giving our vessel, location and heading. At 75 yards our inboard engine was no longer making headway against an ever-swifter current as the banks narrowed the channel towards the bridge abutments. With inboard and outboard engines at full throttle *Ibis* inched toward the bridge. At the stroke of 7 o'clock the bascule slowly started to lift and by the time it was fully raised we had 25 yards to go. We were starting to congratulate one another on our perfect timing when a loud clanking sound above us signaled that the bridge tender had already started to lower the bascule above us. In complete disbelief at his disdain

for our predicament, we were unceremoniously forced to cut the engines and drift downstream to a safe distance. There we anchored, brewed some tea, and waited out the hour for the 8am opening while the bridge tender no doubt enjoyed himself. This was probably not the first time he had watched this unfold and it likely will not be the last. I passed the time engrossed in Plummer's *The Boy, Me and the Cat* to find that our little setback was a mere bagatelle in comparison to those that he and his son endured.

One evening we anchored for the night on Moon River, renamed from Back River by the Georgia legislature in honor of native son and Hollywood lyricist, Johnny Mercer. Even at sundown, the solar shower, suspended from the boom, provided copious amounts of surprisingly hot water. After the Captain's fine chicken pot dinner and a little liquid refreshment we retired for the night. I mused over how exotic the song, Moon River, had sounded when I first heard it as a boy growing up near Bristol, England. Bristol, of course, has a long seafaring tradition. It is the origin of the nautical saying "Ship-shape and Bristol fashion" meaning everything aboard is in good working order. Bristol's waterway shares with the ICW opportunities to run aground. It is located several miles up the river Avon where 30 foot tides strand an unwary helmsman tempted to cut too sharply across the inside bend of the winding muddy river. With that caveat to self I drifted asleep.

Some have noted that a consequence of getting older is that one's bladder capacity is not what it once was, a condition I came to find I shared with the Captain. An alternative hypothesis, of course, is the presence of the grog dispensed from the ship's spirit room "for postprandial relaxation." But be that as it may, when nature calls aboard *Ibis* at night, she sets off a set of stereotypic responses. Grudgingly rising from one's bunk, a ceiling soon enforces horizontal movement only as one gropes for handholds to reach the hatchway and the vertical parting in its mosquito net. The next move is the most difficult. One has to slither like a snake up the hatchway and then sideways through the gap in the netting. It goes without saying that waking one's shipmate or granting admittance to a single waiting mosquito is considered poor form. Now it so happens that the Captain and I have both had surgery for multiple herniated discs, their demise undoubtedly hastened by the fiercely-contested squash games we played on the Harvard-MIT courts. With little residual motion left in either lower spine we each resembled stick insects, one finely bronzed and the other as pale as the moon, emerging slowly and carefully through the hatchway netting to take care of business, before painstakingly reversing each step to spend the rest of the night in blissful peace.

James Asheton-Miller
Ann Arbor, Michigan

Apparently I succeeded last week in:

1) Taking some photos with the digital camera
2) Getting them onto the computer
3) Attaching them.
4) Successfully transmitting them to you

I'll try now again.
Gale warnings are up for tomorrow. So it should be interesting.
Until next time,

Fair winds and fond wishes,
Roland

Chapter 7
Seven O

May 7th

McClellanville, SC

Dear family and friends,

And greetings from the coast of South Carolina.

James departed *Ibis*, Charleston, and me on Saturday back to Ann Arbor.

Alan Lewis flew in laden with elegant, frozen, prepared meals from a fine Boston restaurant. He also brought along a last-minute companion, our adventuresome friend Bob Weiler. Just how *Ibis* will accommodate *three* six-footers remains to be seen. Should be interesting. We were off by noon.

We crossed Charleston Harbor under calm conditions with sail up, and found our way back into the Intracoastal Waterway. Motored until 6pm, about 24 miles, to a muddy anchorage in Awendaw. Bob announced, after less than a day aboard, that he needed to board a plane out of Charleston early the next morning for some consulting in New York. So we scurried about, scanned the shores and identified a promising early-morning landing spot. Secured permission-in-advance from a woman fishing with a little boy on a pier. Bob then arranged to be met here in the wee hours of darkness by a driver for his ride back to Charleston.

You might wonder why Bob flew down from Boston to Charleston for a half day on this ICW cruise. I found out.

Bob, Roland and Alan: "boys' night on the town."

To create and attend … a Party. My 70th Birthday Party! Much unaccustomed, scrumptious, imported food. Too much wine, too much bourbon, too much Captain Morgan Rum, and lots of hilarity and howls late into the swampy night. It was the ultimate "boys' night on the town!" No finer way to begin to celebrate the turn of the odometer to Seven O than aboard ship with dear friends.

Five-thirty came too soon for the grogged and groggy mariners. We arose, partially awake, hauled anchor and, with the aid of the compass, and under cover of darkness, successfully found the appointed dock at the appointed time. Like a clandestine U.S.

Navy Seal operation, we dropped Bob off without a dog barking or a gunshot. He had somehow withstood our slumber party curled up in the 5-foot cockpit (in the rain of course). However, because his driver was unable to find him here along the remote ICW, Bob had to lug his wet, 80-pound backpack with his consulting papers and costume (in the rain of course) 5 miles to the Seaweed Grill for his pick up. Made his plane, though.

Here's what Bob can remember about the boys' night on the town:

> Have you ever invited yourself to a Birthday Party? I have. Alan and I arrived in Charleston to take on the Town, a boat, and a skipper we loved. Prior adventures together in far off places had already exhausted most of our youth. But not all of it.
>
> We found the Charleston City Marina, one of the largest along the entire Intracoastal Waterway. After some searching, we also found one of the smallest vessels along the waterway. Our 204-inch auxiliary yacht, hidden among more proper yachts, awaited only provisions.
>
> Rum is the primary fluid for propelling both sailing vessels and skippers. We had heard that this skipper had been without for many a tide so we boarded with gallons of Captain Morgan. And, of course, our ready-to-eat, old, new, fresh, frozen, northern and southern sweet food delight.
>
> The bilges thus handsomely stocked, we set sail across Charleston Harbor with our faithful skipper. True sailors will tell you that the only reason some people call themselves "blue water sailors" is that they don't know how to anchor. We turned out to be blue water sailors.
>
> At around dusk we started looking for an anchorage. Finally, with the help of a shoreline neighbor, horrified to see a boat and three scruffy sailors parked at her dock, we identified both an anchorage and a place to offload me the next morning. We thought the shoulder of the ICW perfect and dropped the hook in three feet of muddy water. Whereupon, huge bugs, winds, waves and oncoming boat traffic suddenly interrupted our evening. We ably addressed these inconveniences by

breaking out the rum to celebrate our captain's 70th birthday. Toasts to the boat, to the fine anchorage, to our navigational abilities, our friend on shore, and to one another.

Then we opened, thawed, chopped, cooked, burned and ate our eight-course supper. Scraped and kinda washed the pot. And, once again, joined Captain Morgan in toasting our heroic accomplishments.

Slept some.
It rained.
We were almost run over by a tug.
Awoke at zero dark thirty.
Sailed, rowed, walked back to the woman's lawn.
I was dropped/thrown off.
Walked, ran, thumbed, found a ride almost to another state.
Got to the Airport.
Flew to New York.
All in 24 hours.
Good night! I would say so.

Bob Weiler
Camden, Maine

Alan and I reset the anchor and anchor light and got some more sleep. Then motored into the wind about 15 miles until about noon when strong northerlies on the nose drove us into the arms of McClellanville, South Carolina. Here we discovered, serendipitously, a charming, unspoiled, indigenous little harbor with a seedy, crumbling "marina" identified by a scruffy sign as "The Devils Den." Happily, the rotten, splintery dock offered good cover from the north and from the approaching gale. And here we are currently holed up, probably for several days, as a very strong tropical depression blasts through. Forecast is 40-50 knot winds and rains. 20-30 knots already. [I later learned that during this blow a 55-foot ketch sank with all hands off the South Carolina Coast. Not far away.] I'm glad we're in the waterway and not *out there*.

The marina is without improvements but the flush flushes and the shower showers. And the "pool" offers three feet of muddy water at low, with only a few alligators. And we are in a safe lee.

Rains are supposed to begin Wednesday into Thursday. So Friday may be the first ICW day. This is a test of our ability to sleep, read, walk, explore and generally live the life of tourists. So far we are passing. And it's great fun to be with Alan and catch up. His lifetime as a travel company CEO promises to show itself to great advantage.

More to come,

Fair winds and fond wishes,
Roland

Chapter 8
Tourists Ashore

May sometime

Still in McClellanville

Dear family and friends,

Heavy rains and 20-50 knot winds have punctuated our 5-day layover in McClellanville while we weather the weather. Thankfully, Alan and I and *Ibis* have been tied up at a salty marina with good cover and remain undamaged and undeterred by the gale. And what threatened to be a "lemon" Alan has transformed into delightful sweet southern tea.

We have been walking and thoroughly exploring this sleepy little town. The rough roads and paths take us beneath live oaks laden with Spanish moss. One stroll revealed a stunning, 1000-year-old oak. Not an ancient redwood, but that's an old tree! We paused to admire the local fleet of a dozen weathered shrimp boats that goes out soon to begin their season. But, like us, even they may be deterred by this storm.

One amusing highlight was Alan being chased by a woman with a broom who thought he was a developer. Alas, our "marina," which we are coming to hold with considerable affection, is scheduled for a locally unwelcome development. Alan has befriended, in this lovely little historic town, many denizens from fishhouse workers to shrimpers to our dockmaster Duane. All without brooms! His background in travel renders him completely at ease in cross-cultural settings, of which this is certainly one for us.

We have eaten royally at local restaurants, always including crab, shrimp, and oysters … usually fried. Our last night at the *Buckshot*, a soul food place, loaded us up with deep-fried everything: fish, shrimp, oysters and okra. It will take a while and lots of bran to purge the systems!

Prior to the Civil War, this part of South Carolina produced about half the country's rice. So Alan commandeered a tattered car, and with highway visible through the floorboards, we visited two rice plantations. Each presented remarkably beautiful avenues of oaks and moss with elegant "big houses," juxtaposed with tiny, austere slave cabins. One plantation offered a most unusual presentation in Gullah, the language of the slaves in this area. Gullah is a mix of West African and a half-dozen other languages. It's still spoken by some 50,000 African Americans in coastal South Carolina. Not easy for these Yankees … or anyone else … to understand!

We drove to the Rice Museum in Georgetown. Georgetown, Beaufort and Charleston are the three lovely old antebellum cities of coastal South Carolina. Somehow each managed to escape the wrath of Union troops … and subsequently of developers.

We took a trolley ride to view historic Georgetown homes. After a time slumbering through a tedious monologue from the driver, we jumped ship to set out on a more lively, self-conducted tour of our own. Alan has very high standards for tour guides!

It was great to have so much time with Cousin Alan. He is the best tour guide imaginable. His humor, generosity, daring, playfulness and travel savvy made for a very special week. I have been blessed by wonderful crewmembers … afloat and ashore.

My cousin, often a man of few words, offered: "Roland, a trip to remember!"

Alan and Roland and the Devil's Den. Photo by Duane.

Although it has been a week of only 40 miles traveled on the ICW, it has offered my longest opportunity of this trip to be outside of *Ibis* and inside a local culture. Well worth the layover at the Devil's Den. Were it not for tropical storm Andrea, I would never have had the gift of this intimate look at rural, coastal South Carolina.

I feel especially fortunate to be seeing places like McClellanville before gentrification washes away their charm and historic identity. In a few years one will be unable to enjoy this experience, as the building boom I am seeing in the Keys now extends all the way up the coast. Outsiders are buying up "hundred dollar dwellings on million dollar sites," tearing them down, and putting up one McMansion after another.

Thank you for a wild, windy, wet one, Andrea! Now let's see some fair winds!

Fond wishes,
Roland

Chapter 9
Under Way ... Again

May 10th

Lockwood's Folly Inlet, NC

Dear family and friends,

Up early and set out from McClellanville. Left Alan on the sagging dock of The Devils Den with his arm around our salty dockmaster. He was heading back to Charleston and thence to Boston. I'm on my own again. A different feeling: considerable excitement ... and apprehension.

The gods of the winds and currents, so favorable for so long, have turned against *Ibis* and me. Tropical depression Andrea left 20-25 knot northwest winds in her wake ... and on our nose. And then there are the tides and currents. The tides up the coast are intriguing: 1-3 feet in Florida, 3-4 feet in Georgia, and 8-9 feet here in South Carolina. You don't want to buck a tide in a small, low-powered vessel for very long in South Carolina. In these narrow creeks and cuts they usually win! Couple 'em with headwinds and they *always* win.

Ibis and I motored into both current and wind until noon. Then decided to hang it up in Minim Creek, a little shoot off the ICW. It was a long, short day ... 12 miles in five hours ... about 2 ½ knot average. Life is too short for more of this stuff! Minim Creek is the last anchorage before encountering the huge Winyah Bay. Four 30-some foot sailboats came in later with the same in mind. Will get on the bay early tomorrow morning at low tide and plan to ride the tide up.

I took advantage of a favorable afternoon of unfavorable conditions to clean, sort and organize the entire boat. And to reflect on what has now become, of necessity, my evening, routinized ritual:

- Get anchor down and anchor light up.
- Savor a glass of merlot and begin recovery from the day.
- Feast on an increasingly familiar 'dinnah': chicken, periodically cooked or purchased cooked ahead in bulk. Rice. With spinach salad. Spinach keeps longer with minimal refrigeration than lettuce!
- A cookie.
- Clean up the dishes, the boat, and sometimes, myself.
- Rig the mosquito netting.
- Go below and record in the logbook major (some would say minor) events of the day.
- Listen to the marine weather forecast for the morrow. Smile ... or grimace.
- Read the cruising guides and see what intelligence, if any, they have to offer on the forthcoming chunk of the ICW.
- Study carefully *The Intracoastal Waterway Chartbook: Norfolk, Virginia to Miami, Florida,* by John and Leslie Kettlewell. This remarkable resource is a small, handy, spiral bound, AAA-like TripTik that presents in fine grain every detail of the 1065 mile waterway from Miami to Norfolk.
- Note troublesome spots like bridges, junctions in the ICW, inlets and large bodies of water to cross.
- Find and label four or five promising anchorages over the next 50 miles so I will have ready options, no matter what conditions arise and how far I am able to get. (And consider what it must be like on one of those hundreds of powerboats I see

each day that set out to go someplace … and then go there!)
- Finally, if tomorrow's "troublesome spots" and winds and currents dictate, set the alarm accordingly for a darkened awakening.
- Get breakfast and clothing laid out.
- Thence to the welcome and welcoming bunk for 5-10 hours of tossing and turning while dreaming of those troublesome spots. With an ear for wind shifts, signs of dragging, keel on ground, or bumping of another boat.

That's the ritual. Especially crucial when sailing alone. There will be little opportunity to do any of this while underway. I have discovered a centipede I am not!

Mosquitoes last night were right up there with the worst I've seen in the Florida Everglades, in grandeur, number and velocity. Somehow, about 500 got in. I killed 490. The other ten tormented me throughout the night. Applied bug spray while in the now-saturated sleeping bag. That helped. In the morning the ceiling of *Ibis* looked like a bad case of chickenpox!

Motored into fog and light northeast winds. Passed abeam of an alligator swimming along the bank of the Tom Yawkey Wildlife Sanctuary. Gives new meaning to "Yawkey Way" for this Red Sox fan. At first I thought it was a log but the wake was flowing the wrong direction. No dips today.

Motor-sailed Winyah Bay without incident with excellent wind and current conditions. Fog wasn't as impenetrable as that on the coast of Maine but the GPS brought welcome assurance nonetheless.

I found comfort upon entering the beautiful Waccamaw River … the prettiest stretch of the ICW to date. Cypress replace palms. Most of this is wildlife preserve and swamp, so I encountered blessed few buildings, marinas, boats, and signs of mankind. Tasted the water: *fresh*! About the color of coffee … Starbucks Breakfast Blend. The Waccamaw is like sailing on a beautiful chain of Maine lakes adorned with water lilies, woods, and peacefulness. I expected to see an Ivory-billed Woodpecker at any moment!

Anchored in a corner of the cypress swamp just off the ICW, after traveling 41 miles in 10 hours. Nearby is Bucksport, named by one James Buck, a Mainer who came down looking for shipbuilding lumber. He also named the town in Maine. Went for a kayak paddle, watchful of any alligators larger than my 8-foot vessel.

Nearby were two Alberg 37's. The owners invited me on board for a drink. They're heading for the Potomac. Gave me their "boat cards" in case I want to stop over as I pass through. Every vessel seems to have designed a unique calling card with the boat's name, picture, and phone numbers. I don't think I'll go there. A bit pretentious for a 17-foot catboat, wouldn't you say?

A disquieting night's sleep with some of the eeriest sounds I ever want to hear emanating from the swamp. Glad I'm not shipwrecked in there! Or was it but another haunting dream?

If yesterday was the best, this day became one of the worst of the trip. Entered the "rockpile," a stretch of about 30 miles of a very narrow, straight, forgettable canal. The Army Corps of Engineers finished this section of the ICW last, in 1936. The Corps left chunks of rock along both shores, barely visible at low. When the dreaded powerboats come barreling past, I have to head towards this inhospitable shore as their huge wakes try to impale me on the now- visible and breaking rocks. A powerboat on one side and a rock on the other! Big vessels, speeds, waves and rocks. Small boat.

The moron-of-the-day award goes to a water ski boat that tore down the canal at 40 mph towing not one but two skiers. Then came back the other way for more. No way he could slow down and keep the skiers up. I was working harder at missing them than they were at missing me. At one point it looked like one skier would fly past me to port and the other to starboard! When commercial barges come through you can imagine what that's like. Either way, not much room for the long boom of a catboat hung out on a run. White-knuckle time. This piece of the ICW is one reason the waterway is often referred to as "The Ditch."

Encountered one item of interest in Myrtle Beach, South Carolina. I motored under a cable with gondolas filled with golfers moving across in both directions going from their 18 holes on one side to the clubhouse on the other! Thus sayeth the cruising guide.

Passed over my *third* state line ... into North Carolina!

Put in and anchored behind Lockwood's Folly Inlet near a marina (but of course, not *at* the marina!) Apparently, in the late 1800's Mr. Lockwood constructed a fine sailing schooner here. On her ceremonial, maiden voyage out the inlet to the sea she went aground because draft exceeded depth. The new schooner was unceremoniously demolished by the seas and shoals. A short lifetime for a vessel ... and a sobering warning for the rest of us prone to folly.

The sailing conditions today have been excellent: tides, currents and a light beam breeze. Great ground and water covered, a record 55 miles in 11 hours. When the conditions are there, as they occasionally are, I run out the string until dark cuts it off.

Fair winds and fond wishes,
Roland

Chapter 10
Fear

May 13th

Topsail Beach, NC

Dear family and friends,

Today I passed, not under but *through* a bridge ... a "pontoon" bridge. I thought I had seen them all ... swing bridges, bascule bridges, double bascule bridges, fixed bridges. A pontoon bridge is a floating section of a bridge that is opened by pulling that piece on a cable out of the way so boat traffic can pass through the opening. Opens every hour or so. Therefore lots of traffic. So far North Carolina gets my vote for the most unresponsive bridge tenders. They seldom acknowledge, let alone reply to, a VHF radio call. Makes the approach under sail rather mystifying ... and often hair-raising.

After a good motor to Southport at the mouth of the Cape Fear River, docked at a new marina and checked the passage up the river to the resumption of the protected waterway, about 15 miles further upstream. Inquired of tides (strong), chop (fierce), navigation (well marked), anchorages (none).

Cape Fear, well named, is said to be one of the most dangerous spots on the east coast for boats of all sizes. Its Frying Pan Shoals are as big a graveyard for vessels as the Diamondback Shoals of Cape Hatteras. *The Boy, Me and the Cat* were shipwrecked off the mouth of the Cape Fear River. It was on a sand bar near here, that Henry Plummer, after swamping his dory, totally disassembled and reassembled and restored its old make-or-break engine.

The choices for me appeared to be:

Motor up the river against a 3-4 knot outgoing current the rest of the morning, catch the incoming tide when it turned, around 1pm, then, hopefully, traverse the rest of the river in relatively calm winds before the predicted strong on-the-nose-northerlies picked up later in the afternoon.

Or wait until 1pm when the tide starts in, go with it and hope to make good progress before the northerly sets in.

In retrospect I didn't, but should have, paused over a third alternative, so obvious to my readers: stay in Southport Marina until better conditions presented themselves, i.e. both favorable tides and winds. But better conditions were not on the horizon for the next few days. Many tough judgment calls on this passage and this was one of them.

I chose the first.

I got about ⅓ of the way up the river towards the resumption of the ICW, slogging against the strong tide with those "twin screws." Then, around 1pm, the tide went slack. And at about the same time, as is so often the case, came a big change in winds. The dreaded north winds started smokin' … way early … 20-25 knots, I'd say. Soon, a ferocious chop and sea began to build, as is also common when wind and current are in opposition. Barely held even, with outboard's prop out of water and, like the sail, useless. Lower mounted inboard prop cavitating much of the time as well.

Another unwelcome judgment call: I could turn and head back to Southport with the wind but against the now incoming tide and give back my hard-earned 6 miles. Or find a place to hide. But clearly I couldn't go on. At that time I remember recalling the advice

46

Benjamin Franklin once offered to the delegates of the Constitutional Convention in 1787, "Doubt a little your own infallibility." Timely advice. I doubted more than a little.

The chart showed no anchorage along this section. After more careful scrutiny I identified a little spot between two marshes at the edge of the Cape Fear River. And, with the aid of the GPS, I ducked in, set two anchors … and promptly took a nap.

I was awakened in an hour or so by the boat's violent pitching and rolling. The tide had risen and my lee shore was now under water! I was now anchored out in the middle of an ocean of whitecaps with a few sprouts of marsh grass peeking through. Untenable … again.

Studied the chart and identified by sight a clump of loblolly pines shielding a portion of Walden Creek, a mile to the west. Lifeline and vest on.

Would love to have had a crewmember or two! Got two muddy anchors up, coiled and secured on the wet, pitching deck … with considerable difficulty. Then, on a half tide, motored over what the chart showed as ½ foot depths. Didn't even want to think about how I would get *out* of here! Used both engines against breaking seas, then, into the creek and a most welcome protection in deep water behind that pine grove.

Beautiful evening with hundreds and hundreds of lovely white ibis flying in and out of the marshes. *Ibis* is right at home, for apparently the Cape Fear River hosts about 10 percent of the nation's ibis population.

The accustomed early evening glass of merlot was suddenly interrupted by the roar of the largest jet ski I have ever seen, blasting at high speed out of the serene marshes of Walden Creek. It went past me and, shortly after, returned.

The helmeted driver of this shiny new vessel slowed and motored up alongside. In this totally desolate spot I prepared for a "Deliverance" moment. She (yes, *she*) offered me a ride up the creek on her brand new steed. What to do? Accept, of course!

Ibis and ibis in the marshes along the Cape Fear River.

For one who looks down his nose at powerboats in general, and jet skis in particular, I have to admit I got a huge kick out of rounding those serpentine bends at 40 miles per hour, hanging on to my driver for dear life as her hair streamed in my face. But as we skimmed along, barely touching the water, my lack of basic trust kept telling me that when (and if) I was returned to *Ibis* I would find that the rest of her pirate band had stripped and sunk my boat. Unfamiliar desolation in the backwaters of North Carolina and a day being pounded on the waves do weird things to the minds of stranded mariners.

Happily, it was a most welcome deliverance. The water-jockey's story unfolded. Her husband had been killed in a logging accident weeks before. To help her through her grief she had taken her inheritance, fulfilled a lifetime dream, and purchased the best jet ski money could buy. The new machine, during this break in period, was limited to 40 mph. But in six more hours she would be able to open it all the way up to 60. At which point I gather her grief would vanish. My ride was helping her towards that goal. I'm glad I didn't arrive a week later!

My comely driver told me *Ibis* was the first boat she had ever seen come off the ICW and into the creek. I guess so! On my part, I experienced a number of firsts as well!

Not only did this guardian angel return me safely but then, as dark settled in, she drove me over a protected shortcut from my anchorage back to the river, reentering a couple of miles upstream from my inboard course. And no 6 inch mud flats to worry about. She carefully pointed out a string of red crab trap buoys. These would mark the correct course for me over the twisting passage, come morning. If I could find them again in the dark.

Slept fitfully with 15 eventful miles in 4 ½ hours under my belt … and with 20-30 knot winds whistling in the pines above. New worries surfaced about what conditions the morning would offer for the remaining 9 miles or so of the Cape Fear River. I did know that the tide was high and would start back out on my nose around 7am. It would be another alarm clock wake up call.

A beautiful, crisp 48-degree morning greeted me with the buzzer at 5am. Raised, coiled and lashed the anchor and left Walden Creek in pitch darkness. The plan was to catch the last two hours of favorable, incoming tide and get off the Cape Fear River and into the protected ICW before the again-predicted dreaded northerlies set in.

With the spotlight and compass I was able find those red traps and retrace, without kissing bottom, our route of the evening before … more slowly! Got out into the river and found the north winds already blowing 15 or so knots. *Huge* swells as the winds and tides resumed their collision course. Heaviest seas *Ibis* (and I) ever want to see. Almost turned back into the creek, if I could have found it. But conditions looked less fearsome a couple of miles ahead. At least I could see no whitecaps with the binoculars in the early light of dawn. Rounded a corner of the river and things calmed down to 2-3 foot seas … still a lot of sea in a little boat. Made it out of the river at 7:30am and into the awaiting ICW, where I motored into northerlies the rest of the day. Anchored early at Topsail Beach at 4pm after 39 miles in 10 long hours.

As I sipped a cold one ... two cold ones, actually ... my mind began to take inventory of all the possible ways I'm finding to screw up out here on the water. So many. The likelihood of most of these feared events happening seems to be in direct proportion to the wind velocity: tacking and fouling the main sheet around the outboard; gybing and fouling the sheet around ME; having too much sail up; being swept off the deck by the boom while putting in a reef; going overboard in a big piece of water with no boat or shore in sight; forgetting to don the life jacket; colliding with another vessel or daymarker, hidden behind the sail; sailing a run and having insufficient room to come up into the wind to drop sail; approaching a still-closed bridge under sail and being swept under and dismasted.

Other perils could happen in any wind conditions, of course: faulty navigation; fouling a crab trap with the prop or rudder; going aground; running out of fuel at a critical moment; even choking on a raw carrot. I find myself using on this passage the entire skill set from half a century of sailing, and adding a few more to the repertoire.

The Cape Fear River brought the most fear I have yet experienced on this voyage. Big water. Big wind. Big seas. Big current. Little protection. Little boat.

Fair winds and fond wishes,
Roland

Chapter 11
North to Oriental

May 15th

Oriental, NC

Dear family and friends,

Finally …. a favorable breeze! Started with single reef, on a quarter run. Then winds picked up to 20 or so. With way too much sail up and no cover, I had my first attempt at reefing under sail alone in the waterway. Drove *Ibis* onto a mud flat that offered a bit of lee from the chop if not the wind. Could only hope the tide was coming not going. It didn't matter. In 4 minutes I was able to a) wrestle the sail down, b) remove some battens, c) tie in a double reef, d) refuel the outboard and e) take a pee! And then blow off the muck and back onto the ICW without as much as a muddy foot. Much pleased and relieved by that stop!

South Carolina has its Parris Island Marine Base. Well, today I sailed by North Carolina's Camp Lejeune Marine Base. Saw and heard more military equipment than a day in Baghdad. As one enters a 20-mile stretch of the ICW that borders Camp Lejeune a huge sign with lights warns, "STOP: Live firing in progress when lights are flashing." This beacon gave new meaning to "stoplight." A Coast Guard boat was anchored nearby, in case you didn't get the meaning. Happily, although a military exercise was in progress, the ICW was not closed. Large bore guns shook the air, ground and water, like the strongest 4th of July ordinance in my pyrotechnical career. Osprey vertical take off and landing aircraft appeared as helicopter gunships, and fighter jets screamed overhead.

One terrifying moment arrived with two dark pontoon boats with squads of marines, faces blackened, in full combat gear, steaming right *at* me. No photos! My American ensign flew prominently in the rigging. But somehow, that seemed insufficient protection. Then suddenly, the boats came to a halt beside me, with marines peering from behind menacing 50 caliber machine guns. I thought my days on the waterway were about to end. But, it turned out the United States Marines were merely slowing down to admire this little sailing craft as they passed by. I wish civilians had such boating etiquette. Another half dozen larger assault boats, machine guns mounted, followed but didn't slow for anything!

I enjoyed following seas all the way to Spooner's Creek, a lovely protected anchorage off of huge Bogue Sound. After 54 miles in 11 hours, I was greeted as I entered the creek by a sloop and its lovely crew from New Brunswick, Canada … a couple and two impressive, seafaring kids. They rowed over and introduced themselves as friends of Bill and Marlene Walch. Bill (my next crew) had told them to keep a lookout for me as they moved north from the Bahamas back to Canada. Apparently, we had also been together at opposite ends of Minim Creek some days before. Small world, this Intracoastal Waterway!

The next morning I set out at dawn, just behind the Canadians. The sun was rising earlier every day, as I followed spring northward. But spring also brought with it longer days underway. Winds had blown hard all evening, and now were gusting around 15 knots. Reef early and often! Today decided to double reef at the outset, then proceeded on a quarter run down the remainder of Bogue Sound to Morehead City. Then through a forest of confusing day markers to a new heading of zero degrees, *north*, for the first time since Florida. I reminded myself that Cape Cod is about 800 miles *east* of the Keys, almost a time zone; so much of this trip to date has been easterly and northeasterly.

Happily a strong and favorable current propelled *Ibis* along at a good clip. Predictions for the afternoon were for small craft warnings and winds in the 30's so I hoped to get out of Andrews Creek and across the 5-mile wide-open Neuse River into Oriental before more of those showed up. Sailed down Andrews Creek at the edge of a gybe. Gybed several times anyway, but only once did the main sheet attempt to eject the outboard into the creek! Kissed bottom twice trying to cut some corners in what the chart assured me was 8 feet of water.

When hitting ground, my drill is to harden up on the main sheet, head off, heel over, sit to leeward and hope the reduced draft will see me back into deep(er) water. It usually works.

Only the narrow, marked ICW proper is occasionally dredged, not its shoulders. *Ibis* has a keel and no centerboard or electronic depthfinder, so even with a 2-foot draft, one wanders out of the ICW channel at some risk. It would often have been helpful to have a foot of board down as a depth finder because Geoff's depthfinder-paddle was usually lashed down on deck!

Got to the Neuse ahead of the heavy winds, and went across in convoy with the Canadians with whom I was able to keep up. The *Cruising Guide* says this part of the Neuse (also!) is one of the most dangerous pieces of the ICW, especially in southwest winds ... which were coming. Come to think about it, the *Guide* reports quite a few places as "one of the most dangerous!" As it was, even with winds of 15-20, the seas were rough. But *Ibis* and I made it into Oriental before noon ... to a dock, shower, swim and nap. A most welcome rest stop, after a 30-mile day in 5 ½ hours.

This long and challenging solo ... between the week with Alan and the forthcoming week with Bill ... has given me plenty of time to ponder the stark contrast between sailing with a companion and sailing in solitude.

As is so apparent in this account, I have been blessed with remarkable company for a good deal of the voyage. Someone to converse with. Someone to provide a hand when the two of mine are insufficient. Someone to eat, drink and share the wondrous waterway experience with. Someone to *be* with. Even Henry Plummer had a boy and a cat!

Of course there are down sides for me, as well as for my companion-of-the-week. Sometimes one talks too much when the other would prefer silence. And two people trying to fit, let along live together in the rain or night in a tiny catboat can feel suffocating. Hey, it *is* suffocating.

But the upsides far outweigh the downsides. As Geoff so perceptively, observed these are "… rare opportunities to give voice to opinions, aspirations, and concerns … hitherto discussed with no one."

Which makes the long days and nautical miles I have just spent sailing solo so vivid, by contrast. For a while, observing and fully appreciating a beautiful sunset, a pod of dolphins, or a classic yacht … alone … leaves a sinking, sometimes frightening void. But after a day or two, confined with my own company, I usually work through the transition and find different ways to celebrate, by myself, the magic of the waterway. A glass of wine to toast the sunset. Talking aloud with myself about the problematic bridge ahead. Playing some music on that 70th birthday gift from my family … an iPod! Or kibitzing with other sailors while at anchor, as I have with the Canadians.

Times of stress and distress, confronted alone, are a different matter. Tying a reef in a blow, or docking in a stiff current or getting two anchors, stuck in the mud, off the bottom. These are not merely inconvenient moments but frequently dangerous ones. Dangerous to boat, back, and to others. Under these kinds of conditions it has been impossible to find a suitable substitute for another pair of good hands.

A nice distinction has been made between "loneliness" on one hand and "solitude" on the other. The former is a bad feeling of being alone when you don't want to be alone. The latter is a rather good feeling of being alone when you do want to be alone. I am happy to report that, thus far, when not enjoying companionship, apart from the moments following a mate's departure, I have been enjoying my solitude. Time for reverie, reflection, contemplation, wonderment. Call it what you will, solitude has been another gift of my time on the waterway.

So that, dear reader (if you're still with me!) was a week in the life of this solo-sailor. I hope this account gives you some idea of the variety of water and wind conditions, events, and landfalls I am encountering during this passage ... as well as of the excitement, apprehension, relief, and exhaustion I experience "out there." You can see why this rest stop in Oriental is so welcome.

Fair winds and fond wishes,
Roland

Chapter 12
1000 Miles

May 18th

Oriental, NC

Dear family and friends,

It is raining and I have some welcome time and much to report. I want to try to give you some idea of the rhythm into which I have fallen. I may even be able to do a spell-check for a change!

I am at a marina motel room here in "North Carolina's Sailing Capital," a charming little town of 800 with 2700 registered boats. I'm here for many reasons.

To mark two long-distance milestones:

First, *Ibis* and I (with the help of heroic crewmembers Barbara, Geoff, James, Bob and Alan) have traveled just 1000 miles from the Florida Keys. That's a marker worthy of celebrating.

Second, as of today, I have traveled a distance of just 70 years since arriving on the planet back on May 18, 1937. Another marker of some note for me. And a motivator for this journey.

There are other important reasons for putting in here for 2 ½ days.

My new crewmember, Bill Walch, is arriving (with a retinue of lovely drivers) from Boston. We expect to set sail tomorrow morning and hope to make Virginia during his five days, maybe even the Chesapeake. Bill has already been a most obliging crewmember. "Tell me where you are tied up and we will drive from Boston to there." That gives a captain lots to work with!

I came in off the Neuse River Wednesday morning. That afternoon the weather turned mean. The river was transformed into a very lumpy field of whitecaps in 30 knots of wind. Today it's small craft warnings with north winds. So a good time as well as place to lay over.

Speaking of the place: I was influenced to dock here by my reliable ICW guide book, *Cruising Guide to Coastal North Carolina*: "Very handy indeed if it's time to rest on a berth that does not move with wind and wave. You simply cannot do better than to coil your lines at Oriental Marina whether for an overnight stay or a week's stop."

And then there is the matter of recharging batteries ... literally and figuratively.

Typically they include the ship's battery, depleted by engine starts, GPS and nights of anchor lights and spotlights. And the batteries from an assortment of electronic devices aboard from electric razor to cell phone to computer.

And then, of course, the run-down batteries of the skipper. It has been a week of solo sailing since I left Alan on the dock in McClellanville, South Carolina. That's a lot of heightened attention to day markers, sail trim at the edge of a gybe, tending engines, and handling the wakes of hundreds of boats passing from both directions, sometimes simultaneously. Not enough hands. "You look," as the dock master greeting me in North Carolinian offered, "tarred."

I celebrated my safe passage by immediately taking a hot shower, a swim and a nap. I have never experienced greater joy than lying on a real bed with the window open a crack, experiencing a gale of wind howling outside, with *Ibis* tied safely to the dock ... and falling off to sleep!

I continued my battery charging with meals out (soft shelled crabs) and three showers a day. I uncovered *skin* this morning beneath the layers of sun tan lotion and grime. And afternoon naps. This battery will reach fully charged this afternoon when I go for a massage, a most welcome birthday present for my bad back.

Another reason for the layover is to care for my trusty little 6 hp Suzuki outboard that has seen hours and hours and hours of steady, dependable use during these 1000 miles. Oil change, gear lube change, and spark plug change. I hope this will keep it (and me) going to Cape Cod.

And there is the provisioning for Bill and our five upcoming days … ice, food, fuel, water. And a newspaper to learn that the Sox are 8 ½ games up on the Yankees!

And finally the clean up: of laundry, dishes, *Ibis*, and me.

1000 miles down, about 1200 to go. That's almost half way. No better birthday present!

And now lots of big, open waters ahead: Pamlico Sound, Pamlico River, Albemarle Sound, the Chesapeake, Delaware Bay and on to …

Bill and Marlene and Judy and Nancy arrived and we all held a lively, two-part 70th birthday party, my second of the journey. Part I was in *Ibis'* cockpit: champagne and a stunning bouquet of flowers, all arranged remotely by daughters Joanna and Carolyn and by Barbara. Part II was being treated by my guests to a splendid dinner of local crab, fish, shrimp and other goodies at a charming, local restaurant. In 70 years, I've never experienced a birthday like it!

The next morning Bill's companions set off to play and tour the North Carolina/Virginia area for five days before picking Bill up "wherever you are."

And Bill and I set out for a very different five days. First thick *fog* of the trip, which happily soon dissipated. When it lifted, we motored and sailed the Neuse River, the Bay River, across the Pamlico River up the Pungo River into Upper Darby Creek, and an idyllic anchorage. The merlot tasted especially fragrant after 50 miles in 10 hours.

The market in Oriental had offered no ready barbequed chicken so we had procured a ham. Thus, supper was welcomely unusual for me: ham/pasta/spinach salad and a cookie. But it wouldn't be different for Bill as this would be our menu for four nights. No matter. Bill was a very ebullient, appreciative consumer!

Bill, sunset and Upper Darby Creek.

The next morning we motor sailed, for 22 miles, the Pungo River and Alligator River Canal. Gusty winds astern made for a lively run. Entered the *huge* Alligator River, which felt like Lake Michigan. Sailed in a reefed 15 knot beam reach and finally reached the bridge at the south shore of Albemarle Sound. Entered the marina there for fuel.

Bill and I, depleted after 50 miles in 11 hours on a very unstable run downwind, dropped anchor at the mouth of the river and base of Albemarle Sound. Coming up was a piece of water called by many, along with the Cape Fear River and Neuse River, "the most dangerous along the ICW." I had been reading about this sound for months and so had plenty of time to build apprehension.

The next morning we were up at 4:30am and gulped breakfast. Bill raised anchor out of the mud and we began, with running lights and GPS, the 16-mile crossing of Albemarle Sound. Conditions were mercifully ideal, as we had hoped they might be at this hour: 15-knot beam reach with a few whitecaps as the sun rose. No shore visible from the middle of the sound. I'd hate to be out here in a blow. Got across just as the wind shifted and strengthened to north, on the nose, and seas began to build.

Motored and sailed up to the charming town of Elizabeth City. Thence motored the beautiful Pasquotank River to the much-anticipated Great Dismal Swamp. Legend has it that a surveyor, one George Washington, laid out this canal in the 1700's to connect the Chesapeake with Albemarle Sound. Labor was provided by his (and others') slaves. It is long and straight with a former towpath along the side. Offers lots of downed trees and floating logs and perhaps six feet of unreliable depth, depending upon recent rains.

Entered the first canal lock, and my first ever. Needed instructions from Bill on how it all works: "Do *not* cleat bow and stern lines to the deck as the water level in the lock drops. Otherwise you will loose both cleat and deck!" Took a walk at the rest area where we tied up for the night with 52 miles in 11 hours under our keel.

In the morning we left the pilings and finished the 28-mile swamp, a heroic accomplishment by those unfortunate slaves, but a disappointment to us. Busy Virginia Rt. 17 closely parallels the Canal and diminishes the remote, "dismal" atmosphere a bit!

Exited our second lock and motored into the Elizabeth River and thence through the Portsmouth and Norfolk Naval bases. I found this passage overwhelming. Little *Ibis* felt even more insignificant than she already was, juxtaposed with huge carriers, subs, and destroyers. Armed patrol boats always maintained course between the docked naval vessels and us. First time *Ibis* has been seen as lethal to anyone this trip! Nevertheless, a lethal reminder to stay on course. We've seen a lot of military bases on this trip! And a lot of lethal reminders.

Motor-sailed 5 miles across to Hampton Roads anchorage, one of the roughest pieces of water I've experienced to date. Four to five foot seas augmented by the wake of huge ships. Good to have Bill aboard! Life jackets were on. Got into a welcome but unexceptional anchorage after 43 miles in 9 hours. We (Bill actually) had to relocate the anchor in the middle of the night a record-setting *three* times to find a flat night's sleep. In his PJ's he set the last anchor at 2am. Mud and PJ's and sleeping bags! What a mix.

In the morning we entered southern Chesapeake Bay and motored, and then sailed with full sail up for the first time in weeks. When winds shifted to a run in heavy seas and threatened a gybe, we just motored. Arrived at Cockrell Creek in Reedville, Virginia after 11 ½ hours and 56 miles to another very salty marina. Had a concluding, celebratory dinner of soft shell crabs with Bill and the good women who had come to retrieve him. We were glad to see them. They were glad to see us, as well. Then we went our separate ways.

Here's what Bill has to say about our journey together:

> When we cast off from Oriental, North Carolina in a light rain, I wasn't sure whether I was among the privileged elite to have been selected for an adventure, or the only one dumb enough to have accepted. I'd just committed to five days aboard a seventeen-foot catboat with a salty captain driving himself, *Ibis* and the crew ... me ... at a pace of fifty miles a day. I second-guessed myself, wondering what purpose could be gained by taking time to do this.
>
> Four days later we were on a broad reach across Hampton Roads. That great catboat sail and boom angled wide to port in twelve, maybe thirteen knots of wind. The seas were short, current-piled to three to four feet, the biggest Roland had encountered so far in his journey. Roland steered *Ibis* as a handler holds the bridle, feels the nervousness and steadies an unruly mare; she'd try to slew her rear around, but he'd firmly keep her calm and heading the way she needed to go. We were focused on the seas, ships, heading, heel, wind, waning sun and reaching the night's anchorage and nothing else.
>
> The entire voyage was a pared life. The simplicity of a cooler edited out the complexity of on-board refrigeration. A repetitive menu relieved the burden of choice. The shock

cord on the tiller supplanted the electrical driven piston of an autopilot. The Captain's allowance of a small duffle bag for gear selected essentials over fashion. The clear, unambiguous, ultimate destination of Cape Cod gave meaning to the work of sailing and motoring mile after mile. That simple catboat's low freeboard brought the sea, literally, at hand. Its beamy, roomy cockpit showed how little space is needed for spaciousness.

Handling the boat demanded our total attention, yet in its clarity and simplicity it somehow made space for talking, tasting and savoring the wonders of life. *Ibis'* bow cut through the clutter. I discovered the purpose of adventure for the sake of adventure: an overwhelming sense of gratitude. No other rationale is required.

Bill Walch
Charlestown, Massachusetts

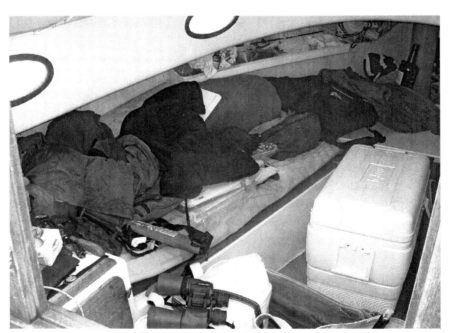

Roland's side: A Third World Country.

Bill and *Ibis* and I covered in five full days an astonishing 250 miles, averaging 50 miles a day, from Oriental, North Carolina to Cockrell Creek/Reedville, Virginia, about ¼ of the way up the Chesapeake. Another very moving passage with great distances covered, experiences experienced, and relationships deepened. Bill, the meticulous skipper of a pristine 34-foot Mason, left me with a parting comment: "Enjoyed the sail Roland, but I have to say, life below with you is like living in a third world country."

Coming up next … a long solo, my third.

Fair winds and fond wishes,
Roland

Chapter 13
The Chesapeake

May 24th

Princess Anne, MD

Dear family and friends,

I am writing from a Wi-Fi site in the town library of Princess Anne, Maryland, about half way up the Eastern Shore of the Chesapeake. I'll be catching the tide out of the Wicomico River in an hour or two so this will be on the brief side.

Why am I way "up the river," about 25 miles east of the Chesapeake channel? I made this excursion in order to stop and visit with good friends, Terrie and Nigel Calder. They lived for many years a half-mile down the road in Head Tide, Maine. Nigel, a sailor and author of some repute, has written on subjects as diverse as repairing diesel engines and cruising Cuba.

Yesterday I sailed across the Chesapeake from Reedville, Virginia at a 15-mile wide narrow portion. Fifteen miles didn't seem trivial to me! Passed Smith Island and ran before the wind several more miles up the Wicomico River.

Chesapeake fishing vessels, Reedville, Virginia.

The Eastern Shore of Maryland is as beautiful and serene as I had heard and expected. Marshes, birds, little islands, old fishing craft and numerous crab traps. A pod of a dozen very playful dolphin cavorted about *Ibis* for 10 minutes. Great fun was had by all.

Long day on the engine, sail … and me. 9 hours. Finally made it into the charming old village of Whitehaven at 6pm, where the Calders have a home. Went aground coming into yet another primitive marina. Rested on the mud until the tide came back in. Then tied off of some pilings in the deeper river.

During my nap, Nigel came aboard to rouse me and say "hello." This morning we toured their new home. And I re-supplied with food, fuel and familiar, good company. *Ibis* and I have covered about 1300 miles with perhaps 900 to go. About 3/5ths of the way! There are no mile markers north of Norfolk (MM 0) so distances from here on will be my best estimates. Winds are southwest now and will be on the nose leaving the river. Weather is looking good for the next few days so I hope to keep going at a good clip. We'll see.

May 28th
Cape May, NJ

At noon on the 25th I left Whitehaven and the Calders and what has to be one of the saltiest, scruffiest marinas on the eastern seaboard. And I am becoming an authority on salty, scruffy marinas! Nary a cleat that wouldn't pull out of the rotten planks in a 5-knot blow! Lots of character though!

Had to dig my way, upwind, back out of the Wicomico River and into the bay. Used the tides and currents to good advantage and sailed a bit when winds turned from southwest to south as we approached the main channel. Anchored for the night in four feet in a wide, deserted creek, well-protected from the predicted light southwest winds. About 20 miles traveled westward today in 5 hours.

Alas, that night around midnight winds came *strong*, perhaps 25 knots, from the southeast and I found myself hopelessly exposed. No other place to hide, so weathered the lumpiest anchorage of my anchoring career. Was not comforted by the absence of visible lights on shore. Pitching so violently, I thought for sure the mast and stem of the catboat would part company. Or the outboard would launch like a space shot from its mount. Set both the Danforth and the plow with full rode. No apparent dragging, although it was difficult to tell. Kayak lashed in the cockpit. Prepared my ditch bag for the first time on this trip.

Unable to sleep or even sustain attachment to the bunk. Yet couldn't sleep or do much of anything huddled and cramped in the bilge. So maintained a watch and waited and tossed until about 4am when things calmed down a bit. Then got a couple of hours of peaceful sleep.

In the morning I found the mast still stepped and the outboard and kayak still with me. And I found no leaks!

Thanks to this nightmare of a night, I was finally able to resolve a conflict that had been troubling me since I left the Keys: Whether to make this trip up the ICW a scenic, tourist event, full of visits to interesting sites and good friends, or to make as many miles each day as conditions allowed towards New England.

After last night, it was an easy call. From here on out, if I expect to reach Cape Cod before snow flies ... *or at all* ... I will forego all future excursions and make miles good towards Buzzards Bay. It helped me reconcile the conflict to promise myself that I will return to scenic spots like Jamestown and nearby Oxford, Maryland, another time ... by *car!* Preferably staying at bed-n- breakfasts from the safety of which I will delight in heavy rains and high winds and foul weather. And preferably with Barbara. So the lumpy night, if miserable and dangerous, proved instructive.

What follows in this account, therefore, may appear at times brisk. It is. It was.

The next day came hot and hazy. Unlike last night, no winds. Motored north with the current at a good clip. Was going to cross over to Annapolis, a town I had always wanted to visit, but decided (given my new resolution) to put in somewhere along the western shore of Kent Island.

Winds making up southwest. Three creeks show on the chart, and no other harbors or anchorages on this leeward shore. I was hopeful one would hold 2 feet of water and good protection for the night. As the sun set I cautiously approached the first and found a sand bar out of water across the mouth.

I went aground in the mud, trying to enter the second creek, going downwind but fortunately with sail furled. Still, the worst kind of grounding. Rather dangerous procedure getting out: going overboard, trying to gain footing on slippery ooze, pushing the transom of the boat to windward while the outboard's three-bladed Cuisinart spun at full tilt a few inches away. And then, when the keel broke free, hopping back aboard before *Ibis* could set out across the Chesapeake

… unmanned. A full gooey mud lathering of *Ibis* and me, and then we were back into deeper (3 feet) water and off again.

It was now almost dark and the southwest winds were picking up on this now unprotected shore. After last night, I wasn't up for another exposed, lumpy anchorage! But I wasn't sure what I would do if the final creek possibility didn't pan out. Three strikes and you're out! Head on up the busy Chesapeake under running lights? Too tired to even think about that. Fingers crossed.

Happily, with more light emanating from the GPS than from the sky, I spied by spotlight, little reflectors on green and red entrance markers. I approached the darkened shore to discover, just inside the creek … lo and behold … a brand new marina, not even finished. Never so happy to find a marina, and a good night's sleep. Fifty miles in 12 hours.

Light southerlies the next morning. Perfect for going up this big bay. Motored under the Annapolis Bridge into the upper Chesapeake. Very hazy and hot with little visibility. Except I could see and smell, all too vividly, hundreds of dead and rotting fish amidst the squalor of the bay waters off Baltimore Harbor. Foulest waters of the trip thus far.

Made 55 miles in 12 hours to the mouth of the Chesapeake and Delaware Canal. Thus concluding, with relief, about 200 miles of Chesapeake Bay … a *big* piece of water for a little sail boat. Blessed by light, favorable winds most of the way.

Put in at Chesapeake City, a tight, snug little anchorage full of cruising boats. Chatted with a couple of other sailboat people about the currents in the canal the next morning. It looked like a 5am departure would catch the last of the strong, favorable current over to the Delaware River.

A huge thunderstorm descended with the darkness. Wind gusts of perhaps 50 knots intruded on the elegant cocktails of the assembly of yachtsmen. Anchors dragged, including mine. Running lights went back on. Out in the torrential rain I went to start the engine, reset the anchor and attempt to fend off other dragging, menacing vessels. *Ibis* and I escaped. Some others did. But many didn't.

A 40-foot sailing ketch and a fancy motor yacht collided next to me like bumper cars. Chips of mahogany and fiberglass flying. Lots of yelling, unkind words, and tempers flying as well from my heretofore-polite boating brotherhood!

Next morning motored under running lights (and streetlight-like lamps along both shores) along the canal at 7 knots, 4 by motor and 3 of current. Traversed the 11 miles of canal to the mouth of the Delaware River. Dodged a few huge tows coming the other way. Don't count on them dodging *you*! I felt like I was riding a bicycle on the Massachusetts Turnpike at rush hour! Much like I have for much of the ICW.

Waited at the mouth of the canal a bit for the incoming tide in the river to subside. It didn't. So set off downstream for Delaware Bay, motoring against a good current. This bay is (also) said to be one of the most dangerous sections of the entire east coast. Shallow waters, a narrow shipping channel, strong currents and frequently contrary winds and heavy chop, wide exposure to the south and east all make for treacherous conditions.

I was much relieved to find an uncharacteristically calm day on Delaware Bay. Little wind and seas. So motored ... and motored and motored. Past a New Jersey atomic power plant. I cowered at the edge of the shipping lane as the nautical 18-wheelers steamed past. As the tide started out, my speed over ground increased slowly from 2 ½ knots up to 6 ½ knots, with no change in engine speed.

Had no hard chart of this bay so relied on my GPS. But it didn't give sufficient resolution in a large scale to plot a course. Called friend and next crewmember, Charley, in New Jersey who called his friend and Catboat Association icon, Bob Reddington. Bob, who has delivered scores of boats along this route, had a chart. Between the three of us we figured out where I could safely leave the shipping channel and strike out across the shallows for the western entrance to the Cape May Canal. Thanks cell phones. And thanks, Bob and Charley!

Faced with the long leg alone down the Delaware River and Bay with some tedious stretches uninterrupted by traffic, day markers or shoals, my mind turned from missing other vessels and being missed by them to more "elevated" conversations with myself. Some call it reflection. Others reverie. In particular, I pondered a paradox: risk and safety.

Sailing is inherently a risky, dangerous enterprise. Out there in a small boat with little engine power, one confronts large rocks and unpredictable winds, currents, seas and other vessels. It is precisely these quite predictable and never-ending dangers that, for centuries, have drawn countless sailors to the water. And now draw me. A boat is safe in harbor, but that's not what a boat is designed for.

So we sailors go out of our way not only to anticipate danger but also frequently to actively court it. For only then can we navigate our way through it. Or not. For you never know for sure whether you'll be able to withstand the challenges that will be thrown at you.

I must confess, there have been many moments on this passage that I have asked, "Why in God's name am I *doing* this?" Well, this perplexing juxtaposition of risk and safety is why I suppose I shipped on for this trip up the Intracoastal Waterway. This is why, as the sun set, I dared the gods by assuming there would be an anchorage for me on Kent Island. This is why I hopped off *Ibis* beside the whirring propeller and pushed her off of the mud. This is why I both looked forward to and feared crossing Delaware Bay today. To see if I could do it. There is, of course, always the possibility that I *couldn't* do it. And this very real possibility is what makes the sailor come alive out there. He never feels more alive than when facing the possibility of death.

Yet, paradoxically, much of my time on the water is occupied by, nay, preoccupied by, a vigilant search for safety. A safe amount of sail up. A safe course plotted. A safe, deep channel. A safe anchor in the mud with a safe amount of scope out. Never have I felt more at risk than in the turbulence of the Cape Fear River. And never have I felt safer ... or more exuberant ... than when I discovered shelter with the *Ibis* in the lee of those pines on Walden Creek.

Even periods of apparent safety can turn suddenly into danger. That "safe," protected nighttime anchorage in the marshes of the

Chesapeake, which turned into a nightmare. That dragging anchor last night in the storm in Chesapeake City which threatening to pulverize me between two behemoths.

Danger and safety. So which do you want? The answer of course is "both." The existence of one gives meaning to the other. Together, they're what life is all about.

After that risky, exhausting crossing of Delaware Bay I tied up at a safe marina in Cape May Harbor at 6pm. Deep water. Cleats hold! Welcome shower. Delaware Bay is *huge* … about 50 miles of it. So today, a total of about 75 miles in 13 hours from Chesapeake City to Cape May, yet another daily record for me. Much relieved to have the Chesapeake and Delaware Bays and this vulnerable solo leg safely behind me. Slept soundly, anticipating fair weather and a crewmember back aboard in the morning.

Fair winds and fond wishes,
Roland

Chapter 14
The Jersey Shore

May 29th

Jackson, NJ

Dear family and friends,

    I provisioned with the usuals: gas, ice and food. Charley came aboard at 6am and we set off along New Jersey's Intracoastal Waterway. Charley and I sail our catboats in the shoal waters of the Florida Everglades. Good preparation for this segment of *really* skinny water. Unlike the ICW to the south, these waters are shallow and narrow and tortuous and seldom dredged. Most boats go outside from Cape May to inlets further up the coast. So no sailboats and very few motor craft in sight. A good thing, as there is precious little room for two vessels to pass, even small ones. We managed lots of inlets, current changes, turns and twists and bridges. Tight going, especially through Atlantic City where we passed abeam of some giant wind turbines. Wind powers all sorts of things!

Charley under wind power, Atlantic City, New Jersey.

As the sun set peacefully, we sailed on and searched for an anchorage in the isolated marshes south of Barnegat Bay. Charley had brought his little GPS chart plotter; I had mine. So we were equipped not only with twin screws but also with twin screens. As darkness descended, we plotted our course, independently. Redundancy is reassuring. Not much room to err. If we agreed, fine. If not, we slowed down, tried to figure out where we were, and then made some judgment calls. One promising anchorage (on the GPS's) behind Little Egg Inlet washed out when the bottom proved too shallow for a low tide and a power cable announced, "no anchoring."

We decided to continue sailing a lovely, favorable breeze under full sail and an almost full moon. Very haunting and lovely. Hunted in vain for what the charts said would be a "flashing green #18." It was nowhere in sight in the darkness ... until we came perilously close by, to discover a menacing, unlit, bent, jagged rusty post . The daymarker had apparently been demolished by an errant (and now, no doubt, badly bruised) vessel. That one could have ruined our whole evening!

We were now in Charley's home waters and happily local knowledge was aboard. Motor sailed into the Beach Haven Yacht Club and tied up for the night around 10pm. Because we arrived well after hours and left well before hours the next morning, we enjoyed not only a complimentary berth for *Ibis* but welcome and free hot showers and a fresh watery bathroom for us. A belated thanks, BHYC!

We had traveled, in 14 hours, fifty miles by line of sight, probably more like 75 on the water. It was my longest day underway to date, breaking the previous all time record of 13 hours set only yesterday.

Back underway at 5:15am the next morning to catch favorable currents. Motor sailing again, as the winds are fluky, if vigorous, in these serpentine marshes. Breakfast underway. Averaged around 5 knots through beautiful, if heavily boated, Barnegat Bay, another piece of water I have always wanted to traverse.

Got a good look at Old Barney, one of the oldest lighthouses in the country, guarding treacherous Barnegat Bay Inlet. A large catboat passed us beam-to-beam, single handed by a 90 year old fellow Charley knows. There may still be a sailing future for this 70 year old after this voyage is over!

Arrived around noon at the venerable Beaton's Boat Yard in the township of Brick. Charley keeps his catboat here and had arranged a neighboring slip for *Ibis* with another neighborly catboater. Beaton's is an impressive, old time operation with perhaps 50 brethren catboats in various stages of preparation for launch. Also on jack stands lay a small fleet of grand, breathtaking A-Cats. Good to be back in gaff rig territory!

I am staying here tonight in Jackson with Charley and his partner Frannie, sleeping on a bed, cleaning up laundry, and writing some e-mails. Charley hosted a cookout with some of his good boating buddies. These included "Mystic" Bob Reddington, supplier of verbal charts to distressed Delaware Bay sailors. And Paul Smith, a wooden boat carpenter at Beaton's, rivaled only by a few gifted craftsmen I know in Maine. It's heartening to see and smell woods, grains, cuts, bevels, sandpaper and varnish in this era of plastic boats.

A good friend of Charley's and Paul's, Harry Sowell, has unexpectedly agreed to pilot me on the next leg. A walk on! Harry is an experienced sailor in waters from New Jersey into Long Island Sound. My first … and only … unplanned crewmember appears at a propitious moment, as *Ibis* heads from here out into the open Atlantic and on up to the challenging East River.

My intent is to rest and reprovision, get the boat beyond a troublesome canal and depart for Sandy Hook and New York Harbor on Friday morning. While this will constitute my first passage into the ocean thus far, at many spots along the way I have been only yards away, separated from the Atlantic by a barrier sandbar. Ah, but what a difference a sandbar makes!

It is about 30 miles from the Manasquan Inlet to Sandy Hook. Then the East River and its very strong currents and Long Island Sound await. Always an adventure around the corner! Cape Cod is getting closer.

Alas, after our lovely dinner party, a major intestinal distress capsized and nearly sank both Charley and me. We both erupted in what can only be described as a tsunami. My only sickness of the entire voyage. But what I did not experience in frequency I experienced in intensity.

In the morning, an Admiralty Inquiry was convened. I argued (rather lamely) that this nighttime, and now daytime, horror must have been caused by the fresh, perhaps unwashed, New Jersey strawberries that Charley had brought on board in Cape May. He argued (more convincingly) that it must have been the slimy, moldy, sliced turkey that had been on board since Charleston … or somewhere … without the benefit of much ice.

In any case it was the most distressing and unpleasant bodily malady either of us want not to recall. The only good news: indoor plumbing! I am beginning to concede that Barbara may have a point about hospital grade hygiene on board.

Here's how Charley recalls those eventful days together:

> I arrived in Cape May with a sleeping bag, a GPS chart plotter and a box of strawberries. Had I known what would

follow I would have included beer, wine and a healthy ration of Jersey Mike's submarine sandwiches.

I began looking for a catboat mast among the hundreds of other boats in the marina. This didn't take long because Roland's was the only catboat and one of the only sailboats to be found.

Roland and *Ibis* looked a little tired from their last few days of their journey through the C & D Canal and down the Delaware River to Cape May. *Ibis* looked particularly weary, what with anchor and lines strewn about the deck, apparently at the ready for any sudden emergency. The mud patina that adorned the deck suggested that Roland and *Ibis* had visited some really great anchorages.

Within the hour we were heading north on the Intracoastal Waterway. Past the Wildwoods, then Surf City and on and on until we came to the railroad bridge that carries the Throng from Philadelphia who hope to hit it big in the casinos.

Resisting the Siren song of the one armed bandits cha-chinging, Roland and I left Atlantic City astern. Our thoughts soon turned to lunch. Lunch! Roland reached into the cabin and pulled out a cooler. Turkey and lettuce sandwiches were made and quickly dispatched. I noticed at the time some water in the bottom of the cooler. I am sure at an earlier time it was in a solid state. This was one of those times that a Jersey Mike's sub would have been welcome.

It was June, and the days were long, so we continued our journey winding through the marshlands of South Jersey. The turns were tight and the waterway narrow. Tall grasses obscured towns in the distance. We talked about our days sailing in Florida and what the rest of Roland's adventure would bring.

It seemed like minutes before, the sun had been high in the sky. But before long we found ourselves peering into two GPS screens in total darkness as we traversed one of the skinniest bodies of water on our whole trip. I detected a little nervousness in Roland's voice but I quickly assured him that we were fine and that he was in the company of a competent pilot. Ha! Had I convinced him, or was he saying to himself, "competent pilot my butt, how did I let him talk me into this?"

It was about 10:00pm, off Long Beach Island that we decided to pull in for the night. Before long we were safely tied up at a dock and taking advantage of the shower and bathroom facilities at the Club.

"Get up Roland, let's get underway before anyone sees us and charges us for our dockage." Roland, being the thrifty person that he is, said, "good plan" and in a wink of an eye, we were once again under way in the darkness.

We sailed under the Manahawkin Bridge then passed Old Barney, the lighthouse that stands at the foot of Barnegat Inlet. Two more hours and we approached the Sea Side Bridge. Again, as Roland's competent pilot, I assured him that we could just clear the fixed west span of the bridge and not have to request a bridge opening. This time, however, he was buying none of it. As the captain of *Ibis* he said, "We'll have the bridge open."

Within the hour we arrived at our destination, Beaton's Boat Yard, a small boat yard little changed in thirty years. Here they still build quality wooden boats, including the famous A-Cats and the Herreshoff Flatfish. My friend Marie Darling provided a slip and it was off to my place for dinner.

To celebrate Roland's safe arrival, my girlfriend Fran and I invited Bob Reddington, Paul Smith and their wives to a barbeque. After steaks, wine and a good desert I went to bed for what I thought was going to be a great night's sleep.

Remember that turkey sandwich? Well, Roland and I suffered and then suffered some more for the next twenty hours. While everyone else reveled in the previous night feast, I spent my time kneeling before the porcelain throne while Roland, a true descendant of royalty, sat *upon* the throne. You get my drift?

The next day, after some initial inertia, we were able to gather ourselves, get to *Ibis* and I sent Roland and Harry Sowell off to the Manasquan River Yacht Club just minutes away from the Manasquan Inlet out to the Atlantic. With my responsibilities concluded, I bid them *bon voyage*.

To Harry my parting words were "don't eat the turkey!"

Charley Best
Jackson, New Jersey

Now, I am content to be ⅔ of the way up the Jersey shore, and comforted to learn that the Red Sox are 14 ½ games up on the nearby Yankees!

More to come. Meantime,

Fair winds and fond wishes,
Roland

Chapter 15
Long Island Sound

June 4th

Stonington, CT

Dear family and friends,

I'm in *New England*!

Where the iris and lilac are in bloom.

Where people *tawhk* the way people are supposed to *tawhk*.

And where every third man, woman or child is sporting a Red Sox cap or shirt!

Stonington is a charming little seacoast town, just as charming as the Stonington in Maine, except with a much better harbor and sheltering far more yachts than lobster boats.

Harry, *Ibis* and I put in to this first class marina yesterday to weather tropical depression Barry (comes after "Andrea"), which as I write this below in the cabin, is howling overhead with gale force winds and heavy rains. The fishermen were bringing in their traps yesterday. It's one of *those* storms.

It has been quite a ride since I last wrote from the New Jersey coast. And it has been especially good to have my new friend Harry aboard. His nautical resume, which includes managing a boatyard, is as impressive as anyone's. His engineering background and precision with navigation have been well employed by this captain, innocent of both precision and technology.

Although I was still a bit washed out from The Bug, we set off and motored *Ibis* from Beaton's Boat Yard through the Point Pleasant Canal to a yacht club at the mouth of the Manasquan Inlet, where Harry had arranged a slip for the night. *Ibis* and I are not accustomed to *yacht clubs*, but could become so! The canal is a particularly nasty bit of narrow water lined by rusty, cast iron abutments and diced with huge currents and lots of traffic. Negotiating it is time-specific. Getting to the ocean side of the canal allowed us to be ready to go early in the morning.

We celebrated June first by "bustin' out all over." We headed out the Manasquan Inlet into the Atlantic Ocean, the furthest north one can go on the "inside" in New Jersey, and indeed on the disappearing Intracoastal Waterway. Passed through the last opening bridge of my voyage after about 200 of them. No regrets.

Harry and Roland heading into the Atlantic. Photo by Charley Best.

I contemplated just how exact and time-bound have been the bridge openings and the tide's comings and goings and how otherwise timeless has been the waterway. For some reason it brought to mind the story of the Maine yachtsman who went into a harborside general store and asked, "Do you have a copy of the New York Times?"

"Do you want yesterday's paper or today's?" replied the storekeeper.

"Well, today's," answered the cultured mariner.

"Then you'll have to come back tomorrow," said the keeper.

Ibis' first open ocean experience was a good one. The winds and seas were gentle and following. We arrived off of Sandy Hook around 3pm, exactly the hour Harry had determined was the most favorable to enter New York Harbor and then, before dark, negotiate the much-respected and anticipated East River.

The winds picked up and we surfed under the Verrazano Bridge ahead of some pretty good seas and into view of the Lower Manhattan skyline. No photos here, as Homeland Security prohibits taking pictures of New York City's bridges. Paused to consider how different it must have been when one Giovanni de Verrazano came through this narrows in 1524, some 483 years ago.

I called my daughter Carolyn who lives in Brooklyn Heights near the Brooklyn Bridge. She had just returned that very day from the hospital with Macey Sophia, her new daughter and my second grandchild. The 70th Birthday Year continues to offer bountiful gifts. Welcome to the planet, Macey! You've been a mariner for 9 months. May many more good years in and on the water lie ahead for you.

New dad Lee was dispatched as emissary to the Promenade where we waved and photographed one another as *Ibis* sailed past ... we thought. Several weeks later, when Lee proudly displayed the cherished photos, we discovered they were of *another* sailboat!

The current in the East River turned strong with us, as Harry and his trusty *Eldridge Tide & Pilot Book* said it would. We flew past the South Street Seaport and dipped our peak to some pretty classy old vessels.

Thence under the Brooklyn Bridge built in the heyday of catboats. Then we admired the Chrysler building and the UN Headquarters as they slipped past. Big city. Big buildings. Big current. Little boat.

My previous GPS-documented speed record with *Ibis* on Florida Bay was 6.8 knots over the ground. I broke that record only last week in the Chesapeake and Delaware Canal with 7.1 knots.

Well, in the East River, with full sail up, outboard running and current boiling, Harry and I and *Ibis* soon broke those records. The GPS recorded first 7.8, then 8.2, and then 8.5 knots! As we entered Hell's Gate, a narrows with particularly turbulent, treacherous, swirling waters, we were transfixed as we watched the GPS record 9.0, then 9.4, then the all-time and new (and doubtless never-to-be-broken) record, 10.0 knots. That's about 11 miles per hour. Not much for a powerboat, but lots for this catboat. The shores went by so fast I can't remember what was on them. I do remember sailing under the landing approach for La Guardia Airport as the jets came in. It seemed we were all flying at the same speed!

As darkness descended, we hung it up for the day at 8pm, just beyond the Throgs Neck Bridge in Little Bay. That was the last bridge of any sort I will go under on this voyage. We anchored, not too close to shore because boaters have reported becoming sporting targets for not very sporting youths ashore. These wayward juveniles delight in bombarding unsuspecting mariners with rocks! But we didn't have to resort to Joshua Slocum's defensive strategy of putting tacks, sharp points up, on deck to ward off nighttime boarders.

The sun went down and the Throgs Neck beautifully illuminated. Our anchor light was deployed to better assist the delinquents with their nighttime fusillade. Thanks to Harry's precise planning of currents and to favorable winds, 65 astonishing miles in one day from the mouth of Manasquan Inlet to the mouth of Long Island Sound!

Here's what Harry has to say about the day:

> Several hours after Manasquan Inlet bid us a calm farewell we were off Sandy Hook with a strong southerly pushing *Ibis* along. I checked the tide tables in *Eldridge* and told Roland we

had a choice – go in behind the Hook and anchor for the night or take advantage of a favorable incoming current and ride it and the strong southerly right through NY harbor. *Ibis*, with a bone in her teeth, answered for us. So we sped along, avoiding the shipping traffic, cutting across Romer Shoal, surfing down the swells that form there (and break in heavy weather), and under the Verrazano Bridge. At this point I was very aware of how small our boat was and ever thankful that we weren't bucking a head wind or a foul tide. A harbor security boat came over to check us out as we cleared the bridge and dutifully noted we weren't a threat to anyone … but ourselves.

Passing Governor's Island, the void where the World Trade Towers once stood and the beautiful sculpture that is lower Manhattan's skyline, all colored by the special lighting of a soon-to-set sun, was a gift that resonated with both of us. As *Ibis* headed up the East River we took in the sights of the Seaport, the resident square riggers, the UN building, keeping close watch on the traffic – the tugs, high speed water taxis and commuter boats, tour boats and small freighters that can make the river seem pretty tight even if you are in a 17' boat. It was here that we broke the all time speed record for a catboat. The stars aligned so that as we passed under the Brooklyn Bridge on our way to Hell's Gate we were given a boost by maximum current and exceeded 10 knots over the bottom. Less than an hour later we anchored in a quiet cove close to the shoreline juxtaposed with the Throgs Neck Bridge and all of its traffic as our neighbor. Captain and crew slept well – even *Ibis* seemed content.

Harry Sowell
Brick, New Jersey

The next morning we were underway at 5:15am with running lights to catch the last of the favorable tide. Ate breakfast as we passed Execution Rock, where capital crime prisoners were once shackled at low tide to be mercilessly dispatched by high. Then we entered the heavily polluted western sound. Not as ripe as the upper Chesapeake but right up there. Long Island soon vanished in the haze and the Connecticut shore and cleaner waters began to unfold.

We passed New Haven Light mid afternoon. Decided to take advantage of a late afternoon beam-reach breeze and favorable current to continue sailing down the sound and up the Connecticut coast. Saw lots of 7.0 speeds as daylight drew down. We decided to make for Westbrook and Pilot's Point Marina where the cell phone told us the fuel dock would be open until 7pm. Crucial to us for the planned early morning departure tomorrow. Tied up at the fuel dock with 20 minutes to spare!

Fourteen hours of sailing and motor sailing and 80 miles covered. That's a lot of miles and yet *another* daily record that I doubt I will ever match. But that's what I thought after the 75 miles down Delaware Bay. It seems that these uncommon, unattainable distances are becoming more and more common. Big miles. Big hours. Little boat. I feel incredibly fortunate to be the recipient of these continuing gifts from the sea gods.

After a welcome shower we went out and celebrated with some equally welcome local seafood to replenish my now-functioning system. And then turned to even more welcome bunks.

Harry (and the tide tables) forecast 2 hours of favorable currents if we got going early; 2 knots against us if we don't. So in the morning we threw off the dock lines at 5am and headed, once again under running lights, for Stonington, 28 miles to the eastward. Light winds and rolling seas. We passed a lovely square-rigged vessel just off Mystic Seaport. It's good to see some vessels older than us! Harry saw his first-ever loon. When the seas flattened we had breakfast and plotted our way through the haze and maze inside Fisher's Island and into this lovely, well protected harbor. The last mile we sailed gently through a very impressive fleet of yachts. Stonington presents like a baby Marblehead or Newport.

After a celebratory beer and lunch aboard with Harry and his friend Linda Fife, another Catboat Association icon [who has recently passed over the bar] we parted company. Linda and Harry set out for the drive back to New Jersey. But not before Harry, with his local knowledge of the New Jersey coast, New York Harbor, the East River and Long Island Sound had piloted *Ibis* some 175 miles in three days. Harry, who has made this passage many times, observed as he departed, "I've never seen better conditions for this passage or made better progress." The gods had been with us thus far ... but an ominous storm was approaching.

Harry at the helm entering Stonington, Connecticut.

After a thorough boat cleanup at the marina, nap, kayak paddle of the yachts, walk through town to admire the lovely old ship-captains' homes, I returned to button up *Ibis* for the blow. Ibis may be the last bird to seek shelter before a storm, but I'm glad this *Ibis* was one of the first! And the rains and winds began. And continue!

This afternoon my good friend Gordon arrived from Maine to accompany me on the last leg of this many-legged cruise. I figure *Ibis* and I have now covered about 2100 water miles. Now less than 100 remain between Stonington and Wareham. I'm beginning to get excited! And it's beginning to sink in that *Ibis* and I may just make it!

I hope the huge seas kicked up by this major tropical storm Barry lie down by tomorrow morning ... when Harry advises leaving at 5am (of course) to catch the last of the favorable currents. Weather predictions for the week, after the storm, look favorable. We'll see.

So that's it from here my friends. Throgs Neck marked the beginning of the sound; Stonington marked the end. So, for the first time in my life I have sailed Long Island Sound from end to end ... all 110 miles of it.

Next, on to Block Island Sound and Buzzards Bay!

Fair winds and fond wishes,
Roland

Chapter 16
The Last Leg

June 5th

Wareham, MA

Dear family and friends,

Gordon, a life-long friend, sailing companion from Maine and another newly-minted 70 year old, arrived Monday by bus and train. Tropical depression Barry was heading off to sea but, because of the 10-foot lingering swells off shore, at 4:30am Tuesday morning we decided without much hesitation not to try to sail up the battered and still turbulent Rhode Island coast. So another day's layover in the lovely, well-protected port of Stonington ... a great walking town. Now three days spent here preparing for weather, weathering and recovering from weather.

Wednesday morning at 4am the marine weather forecast 5-10 knots northwest, an ideal breeze for a gentle beam reach. Small craft warnings for large seas had been lowered as well so we set out at first light, 5am, as I have done every sailing day since the Chesapeake. Our destination was Cuttyhunk Island on the southern end of Buzzards Bay, an enchanting spot both Gordon and I have long relished and neither has visited.

Gordon as sun rises on a "perfect sailing day" off Watch Hill, Rhode Island.

Winds *were* gentle northwest and swells were 3 feet as predicted. Quite tenable. At Point Judith, the only easily accessible harbor on the Rhode Island coast between Watch Hill and Massachusetts, we planned to take stock of the conditions again and decide whether to continue ... or to put in.

After a lovely, clear morning reach under full sail, we came abeam Point Judith and both what we saw and what we heard on the marine weather continued to oblige. The lobster fishermen were all about. To be conservative we put in a single reef and then made the decision to move out across open water to Cuttyhunk.

Alas, an hour later, about 25 miles from our goal, things began to happen. Suddenly. Unpredicted rains began to fall. So we suited up with foul weather gear. Then the swells increased precipitously. We later learned they were 6 feet ... mountains for a little 17-foot boat. Life jackets were donned. Then the winds suddenly shifted to the southwest and increased to 25 knots. A two or three foot opposing chop built on top of the 6-foot swells. Dangerously unstable, confused conditions. Life harnesses snapped in. No photos. Gordon, *Ibis* and I suddenly found ourselves on an unanticipated, unwelcome and fearsome roller coaster run.

Out in open water in heavy seas and winds with too much sail up. These were precisely the conditions I most feared for *Ibis* and had somehow managed to avoid these past two months. And here they were ... on the last leg. No two ways about it, we were woefully exposed out in Rhode Island Sound ... the Atlantic Ocean, really.

I'm not sure where the edge is for *Ibis* but wherever it is we were perilously close to it. She was surfing down the swells as we crashed ahead on a quarter run. We descended, and threatened to broach and rose up again on the following swell.

A single reef presented way too much sail. Yet heading up into the seas and wind and even dropping, let alone double reefing the sail was impossible on the frequently submerged, pitching foredeck. Besides, we desperately needed some sail to stabilize us. So we dropped the peak, scandalizing the mainsail and luffed up a bit and attempted to continue sailing ... and remain upright. "Oh God, thy sea is so large and my boat is so small."

Gordon and I took inventory of our bleak situation: now about 20 miles southwest of Cuttyhunk in open ocean. Newport about the same distance to the west, but into the wind. No land visible in the rain. We'd left the last few fishing boats back at Point Judith. Early June water temperature was in the 40's. An 8-foot single kayak, a meager lifeboat. If conditions worsened ... I'd rather not think about that any more. It was only mildly comforting to hear from Gordon at this time, "Well, Roland, there's no one I'd rather die with than you."

Management consultants tell us that leadership is a foul-weather job. But it's quite literal here. So just what constitutes leadership in this situation?

Decided to put in a call to Barbara, my faithful ground crew during this trip. Managed to rouse her out of a meeting at the Brigham and Women's Hospital and advise her of conditions and location. We agreed that I would call every half hour. If she didn't hear from us ...

well, she had the coordinates. In retrospect, of course, I should have notified the Coast Guard in Newport of our predicament as well. Only in subsequent months have I come to ponder just what it is in the male psyche that cannot confess our folly to ourselves let alone to others, and certainly not to the United States Coast Guard. Let alone ask for help!

After somehow managing to withstand an hour of these unbelievably lethal conditions, teetering on the brink of disaster, things ever so slowly began to improve and become manageable: the rains abated; the winds dropped down to 15 or so and came back around to the beam; and the swells subsided to 3-4 feet.

About 3pm Gordon and I sailed, without engine, into Cuttyhunk's beautiful inner harbor and picked up a mooring. Wasted by turbulent hours in the nautical laundry dryer, we feasted on peanut butter sandwiches … and a celebratory glass of wine. Then the two "ancient mariners" (as Barbara tagged us) took long and peaceful naps! "That which does not destroy us, makes us stronger." Indeed.

Roland on a safe mooring, Cuttyhunk. No more t-shirts and sandals! Photo by Gordon Davis.

This next to the last day of the journey up the coast was without doubt the whitest knuckle of many white-knuckle experiences during the passage. A crashing crescendo, as it were. It's as if the sea god Neptune was saying, "You think you are home free? Not so fast, buddy!"

A cold front blew in that night with more 25-knot breezes. It felt quite good ... as experienced on a mooring from Cuttyhunk's harbor!

The final morning of the trip dawned clear and cool, in the 40's. NOAA promised more 5-10 knot light nor'westerlies. Yeh, right!

We sailed out of the harbor and set a course of 56 degrees straight for Wareham, Massachusetts. It was an unforgettable experience to lay, for the first time, the day's course with me at one end of the rule and my final destination at the other. Then we proceeded to reach briskly across the entire Buzzards Bay ... another first for me. Come afternoon, the winds piped back up to 25 from the southwest, with good-sized rollers making down the bay. We dropped and furled sail and motored the short way up the Wareham River to *Ibis's* place of birth, the Cape Cod Shipbuilding Company. Enough was enough!

Final day, course across Buzzards Bay ... home.

At 3:15pm on June 7th, *Ibis* and I had reached our destination, some eight weeks and three days from departure in the Keys way back on April 9th. Gordon was aboard for only two of those days. But he will remember them. Here's what his aged, porous mind recalls:

> As one views a chart of the east coast of the United States, from the Keys of Florida to the beaches of Cape Cod, the potential for increased adventure and mischief on the water in a small boat clearly increases as one proceeds north to the open Atlantic. And so it was for Roland and me aboard his tiny catboat *Ibis*.
>
> A two-month odyssey such as his required several first mates who could not only stand and withstand Roland for some length of time in tight confines ... a monumental challenge in its own right ... but also form with him a high performing team capable of dealing with comfortable and turbulent conditions, alike. We were about to be tested.
>
> I was the last crewmember and we were on Roland's last leg of the voyage. My leg from Stonington, Connecticut to Wareham, Massachusetts came very close to being *my* last leg as well. Our segment together was divided into two chunks, with a stop at Cuttyhunk in the middle. This portion proved to be the most perilous of his entire trek.
>
> Following a two-day delay in Stonington due to bad weather, we set forth blessed with what were supposed to be much better conditions. Soon we entered the unprotected Block Island Sound. An hour or so out it became evident that NOAA had deceived us, yet again. Well past our point of no return, New England winds and the Atlantic Ocean served up an increasingly alarming pattern of seas. The peak-to-trough height relative to the boat's length came close to pitch-poling *Ibis* and us.
>
> Faced with such violent action, the human mind requires an arresting distraction in order to cope. The Captain and I began to muse on the topic of mortality. *Our* mortality. Not because both of us had recently turned 70, but because we now faced what looked like a life-threatening predicament.

As we elaborated on the topic of death, we reached agreement that each of us could think of no one we would rather expire with than the other. Some consolation.

But not much.

As we began to exhaust this topic, thankfully, the winds and waves began to abate and finally ... finally ... Cuttyhunk came into view.

Our demise would have to wait for another day.

Gordon Davis
Sheepscot, Maine

A most hearty and welcome reception party, Barbara, greeted us as we stepped onto the dock. Absent were the band, bunting, speeches, the press, and throngs of admiring yachtsmen. Present was a wonderful feeling of elation. We *made* it. The final 70th birthday present had been unwrapped and the party was over!

On this entire odyssey I sailed into many sunsets and darknesses but I never once sailed through a night. At the end of every single day of this two-month trip I put in somewhere. Sometimes it was a marina, a dock, more often an anchor. Occasionally I tied *Ibis* to a pier or post or tree. Sometimes it was 4pm; other times 10pm. But at the conclusion of the day I was somewhere. Each day was punctuated by a period.

These destinations were seldom the ones I had set out for that morning. Some came up woefully short, like that anchorage off the Cape Fear River. Others far exceeded my most optimistic hopes, like Charley's and my moonlit 75-mile run to the Beach Haven Yacht Club.

Yet always, these clear and regular bounds to my voyage, these recurring ends stood in unbelievably sharp contrast to the end*less*ness I had usually experienced earlier in the day. Barbara and Geoff's and my legs up the long Florida coast were endless. As Bill and I crossed Albemarle Sound there was a long period when we could see no land in any direction. The sky was endless, the water was endless. The only thing we could see was *Ibis* ... and each other.

And, of course, out in the rain on Block Island Sound, Gordon and I experienced endlessness as well: huge waves breaking endlessly one after the other, uninterrupted by fishing boats or navigation aids. Endless winds and clumps of rockweed whistling past. And, of course, time seemed endless as well. And so it was negotiating the never-ending serpentines of Georgia and South Carolina with James, going up Chesapeake Bay and down the Delaware Bay and the length of Long Island Sound. Endlessness.

The Captain and 1ˢᵗ Rate 1ˢᵗ Mate at Cape Cod Shipbuilding Company. Photo by Gordon Davis.

These daily and dramatic contrasts between clearly delimited ends and unbounded expanses give me much to ponder. Rather parallel with my life's journey. For years, my days and years have seemed endless. Now, the onset of each new limitation clearly lets me know that life is moving relentlessly toward an end. There are many more solid posts to tie up to at the end of more days, I trust, but not as many now as there were when I cast off.

And with that, my friends, let me conclude these *Tales of the Intracoastal Waterway.*

Fair winds and fond wishes,
Roland

Chapter 17
Sea Quill

Afterwards

Boston, MA

Dear family and friends,

I still can't believe that today I'm not anxiously listening to the marine weather and studying tomorrow's charts. It is with a considerable sense of relief, accomplishment, satisfaction, and unanticipated sadness, that I write this last log.

I saw a great name on the transom of a lovely sloop in Stonington: *Sea Quill*. No doubt the name of the vessel owned by a writer. Perhaps his second boat. What follows is the last of my correspondence with you.... a kind of sequel to what has come before.

What to say from a comfortable chair in the South End of Boston, after perhaps 2200 water miles, and many, many weeks, days, hours and moments at sea aboard a small sailing vessel? It will take a long time for this adventure to sink in. Like any lifetime, life-altering experience, it will probably never really "end." To the contrary, I suspect my 70th birthday party will last forever.

Recently I had an unusual experience. I flew on a crystal clear day from Miami to Boston. Whether it was the will of the air traffic controllers or the wisp of meteorology, the American Airlines captain took us almost *exactly* over the entire course that *Ibis* and I had traveled several months before. As I looked below I saw a Google Earth "chart," which complied precisely with the chart of the ICW I had followed for so long and so closely and which remains to this day indelibly etched in my mind.

As we took off from MIA my aerial "map" revealed the string of Keys, Biscayne Bay, the ICW running inside of Miami Beach and on up that endless coast of Florida. Inside Cape Canaveral, across the St. John's River and finally across the state border. I could see clearly the serene, serpentine wanderings of the ICW through the marshes that lay between the huge sounds inside the barrier islands of Georgia and South Carolina. And there was the Savannah River and Charleston Harbor. And then that Cape Fear River. Albemarle and Pamlico Sounds in North Carolina, Norfolk Naval Base and into Chesapeake Bay to Delaware Bay. Cape May, New Jersey and the meandering marshes northward. I even saw the half dozen huge wind generators spinning slowly near Atlantic City as they had when *Ibis*, Charley and I passed them close by. And then Barnegat Bay and the Atlantic Ocean, past Sandy Hook into New York Harbor. The East River into Long Island Sound. And on up to Narragansett Bay as we began to descend into Boston. And then, there was Block Island, Cuttyhunk, and just west of the Cape Cod Canal … the Wareham River!

What, a century ago, had taken Henry Plummer, the boy and the cat some five months to travel and what had taken me 8 ½ weeks, Flight 1506 covered in 2 hours and 55 minutes. Plummer's *Mascot* and my *Ibis* traveled at sea level. The Airbus A320 traveled at 31,000 feet. But all of us covered exactly the same timeless portion of planet earth. Remarkable.

Much to ponder. As I reflect on the experience that *Ibis* and I have recently concluded, aided by some distance… both in terms of weeks past and thousands of feet of altitude, many thoughts, feelings and questions bob quickly to the surface. Allow me to free associate.

It occurs to me that, in the past year or so, I have painstakingly covered the now-familiar passage from South Florida to Cape Cod four times:

Planning my trip
Conducting my trip
Flying over the trip
And now, by writing about it, re-living the trip

What an astonishingly beautiful and varied eastern waterfront this country has. I've seen closely most of the Atlantic inner-seaboard, as only 3-4 knots can provide. Despite man's serious imposition of houses, boats and commerce on these waters, the Intracoastal Waterway remains a national treasure. It is every bit as breathtaking and challenging as I thought it would be when I planned the voyage.

One of my readings on the trip was *A Walk in the Woods*, by Bill Bryson. This is an hilarious and insightful story of two guys who set out to walk the Appalachian Trail from Georgia to Maine … about the same distance, 2200 miles, as I traveled. They arrived in Maine in about the same time of year as I arrived in Wareham.

Lots of wonderful parallels to consider. I calculate, for instance, that I could have *walked* the entire distance from Key Largo to Cape Cod in the amount of time it took me to sail it. There is much to observe at slow speeds. And many mountains to climb and ways to stub your toes.

How many opening bridges did *Ibis* and I pass through after brief, often nervous conversations with their tenders? The guidebooks say nearly 200. That's a lot of VHF conversations.

How many fixed bridges did we pass under, sometimes *barely* under? Considerably more than 200.

We sailed on bays, sounds, rivers, canals, creeks, oceans, inlets, estuaries.… all somehow miraculously connected in one waterway from Tavernier, Florida to Buzzards Bay, Massachusetts.

How many kinds of water passed under this 2-foot keel? Fresh green coming through the Florida Inlets from the ocean; grays in Long Island Sound; hues of brown in the creeks of Georgia and South

Carolina; chocolate black in the Waccamaw River. Sometimes salty, sometimes fresh. Clean in many places, polluted in a few.

And how many gallons of those waters pumped through and cooled *Ibis'* two engines that powered her twin screws? Many. And those water pumps never failed. Hundreds and hundreds of hours we heard the steady purr of the Suzuki 6hp outboard, which demanded no more than an oil change, a gear lube change, and the addition of a few ounces of motor oil. What would Henry Plummer have given for an engine like that?

And how many gallons of fuel did we take on at various marinas up the coast? Not many, really. Perhaps one 55-gallon drum would hold it all. Enough to power one of those many monstrous yachts for a day or two.

And to how many of those marinas did we toss lines and for how many, prepare fenders? Maybe a couple of dozen. From no-rent districts to high-rent ones.

How much do I calculate this trip cost? I never calculate how much matters relating to my boat cost. But certainly little more than $1,000 I'd say, not counting purchase of the outboard and GPS.

And how many major tropical depressions walloped the coast causing us to seek protected shelter? Two: Andrea for 4 days in McClellanville, South Carolina and Barry for 3 days in Stonington, Connecticut.

And how many kinds of weather? From 90 degrees in Florida and the Chesapeake to 46 degrees at Cuttyhunk. No wind, too damn much wind. Fair winds and foul. North, east, west, and south winds. Some, but not much rain. Humid and dry. Clear and hazy. A bit of fog. In 8 ½ weeks out there you see pretty much what nature has to offer... whether you want to or not.

How many times did I raise, drop and furl sail? Enough that my leather sailing gloves are tattered and worn through.

And how many evenings did anchor, chain and nylon go over the side to conclude the day? And how many dark mornings did this gear come out of the muddy ooze and return to coils on deck? Most of 'em.

How many times did I tie a reef or two in the sail? Hundreds. And how many times did I shake them all out and hoist the full rig? Precious few.

How many mornings did the alarm ring before dawn in order to catch the favorable tide or wind or weather? Too many.

And how many 2, 3 and 4-knot currents on the nose did we experience anyway? Discouragingly many of them.

How many chart pages did we turn as we plotted and followed a creek, canal, river, sound, bay, or ocean? Hundreds.

And how many day markers and other navigational aides did we spot and leave to port or starboard? It feels like thousands. I will forever have trouble with "right red return" after a couple of thousand miles of leaving the reds to port and the greens to starboard.

How much time were we powered by sail alone? Perhaps a third. With just engine? Perhaps a third. While motor sailing? Perhaps a third. Drifting or dragging … a bit. How about miles traveled under tow? Happily, despite my new Sea-Tow membership, none.

How many gybes? Too many to count. But, happily, none took the outboard or captain out as that long boom swept across the cockpit.

How many were caused by powerboat wakes? Lots of 'em.

How many powerboat wakes socked *Ibis*? Too damned many. Jerks that cut across the bow or steam alongside and leave humongous wakes are not state specific. These nuts are equally distributed up the coast. The many give the few a bad rap in my book.

How many submerged pilings showed on the charts? Hundreds and hundreds. How many did we hit? None … that I know of.

How many times aground? Perhaps a couple of dozen. Mostly searching cautiously for an anchorage in skinny water. But a few working the boundary of the ICW to avoid the worst of the head currents and wakes. And a few others taking a short cut. Fortunately all the groundings were in varying consistencies of mud.

How many times did my constant companion, the new GPS, bail us out … in the dark, in the fog, in the confusion of intersecting channels, and while anchoring? Many, many, many. Couldn't have made this trip without this essential crewmember. Wouldn't Henry Plummer also have liked a chartplotter aboard?

How many chicken and spinach suppers were purchased, prepared and consumed? I don't know, but it will be a long time before I'm eating spinach and chicken at a restaurant.

And how about all of those bran, banana, honey and tea early-morning breakfasts? I could prepare and consume them with my eyes closed ... which I frequently did.

And how many times did I experience "Neptune's revenge" from my repetitive cuisine and questionable shipboard hygiene? Only once for me ... and once for Charley.

How many other physical breakdowns of this 70-year old body? None, really. Even the fragile back held together nicely, thanks to a good corset and usually successful attempts to employ my head more than my back. It was difficult to maintain much of an exercise regime, however. Nevertheless, I lost 10 pounds during the trip. Maybe money to be made promoting *Roland Barth's Floating Diet*?

And how many breakdowns of the vessel and equipment? Only one split mast hoop in that blow on Rhode Island Sound. I asked *Ibis* to do things that she wasn't designed to do and should never have been expected to do: gybe in heavy air, sail in too big seas and too heavy winds, anchor in huge waves. She did it all ... and more.

How many mosquitoes, no-see-ums, and other unidentified little critters were held at bay by the netting? About half of them it seemed.

So, how many times was the insect repellent applied? In the swamps and marshes of Georgia and South Carolina, once at the cockpit supper, again at bedtime and sometimes on the sleeping bag.

How many times was that anchor light secured under the boom to discourage nighttime collisions? Every night I wasn't at a marina changing crew or hiding from a bad storm. How many nighttime or daytime collisions with other vessels on this "route 1 waterway?" Mercifully, none.

And how many good nights' sleep did this captain enjoy amidst the insects, rains, winds, pitching and rocking, dragging anchors, frightening dreams, and fearful anticipations of the morrow? Precious few.

How many of those clothes in my 1-foot by 2-foot duffel/wardrobe did I need and wear? Perhaps half of them. Although James and I could have used a few more socks.

And how many layers of skin peeled off my knees from scurrying about below? Have a look.

How many fish were caught? None. How many times did I use the rod and reel and trail a line off the transom? None. As Barbara put it, "You have to be an octopus to sail this boat." There never seemed to be an available hand or leg to go fishing, despite numerous fishing boats about.

Of how many states did *Ibis* see the coastline? Florida, Georgia, South Carolina, North Carolina, Virginia, Maryland, Delaware, New Jersey, New York, Connecticut, Rhode Island, and Massachusetts. Only Florida's 450 miles from the Keys to the Georgia border seemed interminable. Rhode Island's was, without question, the most forbidding.

How many days did I sail alone with *Ibis*? I had three solos, one for a half week and two about a week each.

How many crewmembers committed to sail with me? Seven.

How many crewmembers actually showed up and shipped aboard? Nine … counting Bob and Harry.

Somehow, together, we managed to take a boat that was too little for some very big waters and winds and too under- powered for some big currents, headwinds, and distances, and move her, as she moved us, from the Florida Keys to Cape Cod.

So a final testimonial to all of you crewmembers: Barbara, Geoff, James, Alan, Bob, Bill, Charley, Harry and Gordon.

It is no exaggeration to say I couldn't, wouldn't and shouldn't have gone far without all of you. And, in addition to the invaluable contributions made to this passage by relieving me at the helm, permitting me to relieve myself, helping to raise sail and anchor, navigating, making sandwiches, doing dishes, radioing bridges and countless other critical endeavors, there is the interpersonal part. In my time with each of these mates I found my former, rich, relationship immeasurably deepened and strengthened. Even with my wife! The extent of this deepening has been very moving and quite unexpected. Truly another gift of the sea gods.

> If you want to go quickly, go alone.
> If you want to go far, go together.
> *African proverb*

And then there are you, dear family and friends.

The end of endlessness. Photo by Charley Best.

On many Patriots Days I find myself drawn to the Boston Marathon. I've talked with some of those runners who have completed the punishing 26 miles and asked them, "How the hell do you do it?" The most common reply: "I do it because these thousands of spectators *want* me to do it and they cheer me on. I couldn't do it to an empty house."

I have to say the same. Knowing you have been out there in my cheering section, following this adventure on the phone and internet and rootin' me on has enabled me to summons up the commitment, persistence, perseverance, courage discipline ... all those qualities necessary to take on and complete this challenge. I couldn't have surmounted the nautical Heartbreak Hills without you.

I have already been asked, "If you had it to do it over again, knowing what you know now about the ICW, *Ibis*, and about yourself would you have chosen to make this trip?" The answer is most certainly, "Yes!"

If you ask me, "Will I ever do it again ... take a small boat up the Intracoastal Waterway from Florida to New England?" ... the answer is most certainly, "Not on your life!"

So thank you, sea and land based crewmembers, for helping me to fulfill a life-long dream. And for enabling me to celebrate this 70th birthday with a flourish. I look forward to sailing with you again.

Fair winds and fond wishes,
Roland

Cast of Characters

Barbara Bauman, six days
    Key Largo, Florida to North Palm Beach, Florida

Geoff Cooke, seven days
    Vero Beach, Florida to Jekyll Island, Georgia

James Asheton-Miller, six days
    Jekyll Island, Georgia to Charleston, South Carolina

Bob Weiler, one day
    Charleston, South Carolina to Awendaw, South Carolina

Alan Lewis, five days
    Charleston, South Carolina to McClellanville, South Carolina

Bill Walch, five days
    Oriental, North Carolina to Reedville, Virginia

Charley Best, two days
    Cape May, New Jersey to Brick, New Jersey

Harry Sowell, three days
    Manasquan, New Jersey to Stonington, Connecticut

Gordon Davis, two days
    Stonington, Connecticut to Wareham, Massachusetts

Postscript

February 13, 2009

Florida Keys

Dear family and friends,

When I was taking my 70th birthday *cruise* up the Intracoastal Waterway I sent periodic progress reports to friends and family. I am reactivating the ListServ one more time for this final entry into the log.

Last week I attended the 47th Annual Meeting of the Catboat Association, held in Mystic, Connecticut, an event in which I have always wanted to participate. The CBA has about 1600 members around the world and about a sixth of them were present, amidst many catboats, brochures, books, hats, and lively seminars.

Back in 1912, Henry Plummer sailed his 24-foot catboat from Cape Cod to Miami ... and back. He chronicled the trip in a charming little book, *The Boy, Me and the Cat*, with which many of you are familiar. Plummer's passage was a major inspiration for my own.

A few years ago the CBA created, in his honor, the Henry M. Plummer Award.

The Henry M. Plummer Award recipients. Photo by Charlie Ladoulis.

Established on February 11, 2002, the Henry M. Plummer Award will be bestowed to the skipper and the crew who complete a voyage of note such as, but not limited to, that taken by Plummer so long ago, or to commemorate a significant act of seamanship. This award will be presented on occasion as is deemed appropriate by the Awards Committee. While this award encourages catboat skippers to venture far and wide, it is understood that the recipients of this award are expected to have shown good judgment by recognizing that a catboat, by its general design, is primarily a coastal craft and not suited for crossing open ocean. The award is a half model diorama constructed by Henry M. Plummer himself and is a gift to the Catboat Association from the Plummer family.

Award diorama constructed by Henry Plummer in 1912. Photo by Charlie Ladoulis

I am very pleased to report that, at the Awards Ceremony, Barbara and I were presented with this recognition in honor of *Ibis'* eight weeks voyage up the coast. The attached photos show the half model of a catboat and the beaming recipients which we may keep for a year as a reminder of the day and of the trip. Also attached is a photo of the original award, crafted by and depicting Plummer aboard *Mascot* sailing his catboat in Florida waters.

So, I though you might like to know that our adventure together up the coast has been suitably noted in polite society.

As always, I beam up to you from the Florida Keys,

Fair winds and fond wishes,
Roland

About the Author

Roland Sawyer Barth is a consultant to schools, school systems, state departments of education, universities, foundations and businesses in the United States and abroad.

After receiving his Bachelor of Arts degree from Princeton University and Master's and Doctoral degrees in education from Harvard University, he served as a public school teacher and principal for fifteen years in Massachusetts, Connecticut and California.

Barth received a Guggenheim Fellowship in 1976 and joined the faculty at the Harvard Graduate School of Education for thirteen years. During that time, he was Director of the Study on the Harvard Graduate School of Education and Schools, founding Director of the Principals' Center and of the International Network of Principals' Centers, and Senior Lecturer on education. He has been an Academic Visitor at Oxford University and a member of the National Commission on Excellence in Educational Administration.

His particular fields of interest are school leadership, school improvement from within, and the personal and professional development of educators. Central to his thinking is the concept of the school as a community of learners and leaders.

The father of two accomplished daughters, Joanna and Carolyn, Roland Barth is an avid sailor in Maine and Florida salt waters and a dedicated farmer. He and his wife Barbara live in Maine, Florida, and Boston.

Other Titles by
Roland Sawyer Barth

Lessons Learned: Shaping Relationships and the Culture of the Workplace

Learning by Heart

Cruising Rules: Relationships at Sea

Improving Schools from Within: Teachers, Parents, and Principals Can Make the Difference

Run School Run

Open Education and the American School

Breinigsville, PA USA
31 January 2010
231615BV00001B/99/P